MW00936339

DIGITAL MARKETING 2020

GROW YOUR BUSINESS
WITH DIGITAL MARKETING

by **Danny Star**

ISBN: 9781076031402

Dedication

This hard work is dedicated to my daughter Bronson and son Hendrix, for keeping up with my busy schedule, my partner Violet for supporting me on my business journey since 2006. My parents, Frank and Bojana for bringing me up in this world and letting me experience the small business lifestyle as a child, my little brother for letting me lead the brothership. My team members, Nick the right hand man, Robert the bone of the company, Saso for always bidding into new things with a positive attitude. Bobby for believing in me and the business.

Ezekiel for editing and proofreading this book, Alejandra my left hand person, for running the Marketing Department. Elena & Edwin for developing sites for us. Alvin and Marc for creative work. Liz & Morgan for helping our business development department. Daniela & Jazmine for social media management. As well as any other team member of mine at, including countless hardworking interns, former employees, Websites Depot and SEO Academy.

Acknowledgments

To Frederick Vallaeys, Kim Ryne Deis, and Wes Schaffer, Lee Goff, each of whom have shared extensive insights with me to help hone my craft and become what I am today.

They are some of the foremost experts in the digital marketing field and I invite each of you to look into the knowledge they have to offer.

CONTENTS

Preface

The following chapters are meant to share expertise and experience from my numerous years in digital marketing. I encourage all readers to take a look, and I feel that you will find these pages particularly insightful if you seek to study or practice digital marketing as it enters the twenties of this century. Also, if you are just looking to better run your business with gathering additional knowledge about online marketing, to help your business growth this is an ideal read. Hence, students, teachers, marketing agents, freelancers, heads of marketing departments, and business owners will be able to derive a deep value from experiences and advice shared here.

We will cover some of the more effective methods and tools that we as marketers have at our disposal today. Indeed, this is a bit of a renaissance for us, because I can't point to a time in history that marketers had so much potential power in their hands as we do today. Digital marketing is extremely important for business growth as well as keeping the majority businesses in business. Although we'll go over the pillars of methods that help today, keep an open eye out for new tools and new methods in development, because this is a constantly evolving field.

I'll give you an intro to myself and how my life clearly led me into this profession. During my early years, we were seeing the Internet have its coming of age, and it was something that I followed with intense fascination.

We'll then take a look at digital marketing as a whole, and why it's so crucial in the success of today's businesses. Then, let's take a look at ways you can improve your standing amongst your competition. The chapters, in their totality, will serve as a full course for phasing out your development so that you will have a lasting presence and leave a big impression among those you want to discover you. There are potentially millions, or tens of millions of people who will have interest in what you have to offer, so let's make sure they know you're there to give them what they want.

Chapter 1

Introduction
About the Author

There is a quote that I have seen shared widely and relentlessly on millions of social media posts and profiles around the world that says, "Choose a job that you love, and you will never have to work a day in your life." Although this quote is attributed to a Chinese philosopher, Confucius. As it usually happens, especially on the Internet, its origin is open to debate. However, what I am sure about is the fact that this quote very aptly describes my career to date.

My name is Danny Star. Along with being an SEO expert, I am also the founder of Websites Depot Inc., a digital marketing agency founded in Los Angeles. I was born in Slovenia in 1981. While in elementary school, I started programming and coding on Commodore 64. Later, I got involved with CorelDraw when I was assigned to create the yearly magazine of my elementary school. This initial knowledge allowed me to be in charge of a newspaper and a yearbook during my time in high school, from where I graduated in 1999. In the meantime, I also worked for my dad's local publishing and printing company, which was responsible for editing the local weekly newspaper and a monthly magazine that had nationwide circulation in Slovenia.

After starting college, I set up my first marketing company with the aim of promoting local clubs and providing graphic design for business cards and flyers. The first big project that I got was to create local maps of different regions in Slovenia which were to be distributed to Croatian immigrants during the Yugoslavian war. Of course, since this was my first project on such a large scale, I shared this job with my father. During my college years, I was also the president of a local student union, which had its own paper that was published on a quarterly basis.

In Super Senior year of my college in 2004, I was offered a position as vice president of marketing for a European financial institution, which was expanding to the U.S.A. at that time. This gave me the opportunity to step out of my country and move to California the very same year that I was supposed to graduate. Over the course of the next four years, I worked in marketing and finance, which led me to get immersed in the world of Google AdWords (now Google Ads). I was also involved in the development of multiple sites and domains as well as handling various other digital marketing projects.

I always had an entrepreneurial spirit which led to me establishing a successful car dealership that reached five locations in Southern California. While I was running this car dealership and discovering all kinds of new digital marketing tools, I also attended the University of Phoenix, University Duke continuing studies, as well more than handful other online business courses and obtained a multiple certifications business management,online marketing, Google Ads, SEO Courses, Web Design and development and marketing management.

After the economic crisis in 2008, we had to sell the car dealership and move back to the realm of digital marketing, but this time for good. Admittedly, I did not know it then.

What started out as an adventure between me and a couple of friends doing marketing consultation in a small office in Van Nuys, California, eventually turned into a growing full-service digital marketing agency. Since then, Websites Depot has become one of the most important and most respected companies in its industry, with 30 employees and a brilliant reputation. Websites Depot has been a certified Google Partner since 2012, providing digital marketing services that range from search engine optimization and Google Ads management to branding and web development, among many other services. Over the years, I have become a true expert in all things digital marketing and have a genuine interest in technology and all the possibilities that the Internet has to offer.

What Is the Book about?

I decided to write this book with one main objective in mind: to introduce small business owners to the world of digital marketing. This is not to say that this is the sole objective of this book, but it is the reason why I started writing this. However, along the way, there was also a number of other objectives that came into mind. The reason is that I have many close experiences that come with running a small business myself. Things started off gradually. I started off small and tried to turn it big…

Luckily, I was successful. But in doing so, I faced all the problems and challenges that a small business owner faces. Moreover, I saw all the opportunities and ways to grow a small business. Amongst these, one of the most important things that I found to be the key to making or breaking a small business in the modern day and age was having a grip on digital marketing.

Small business owners need to open their eyes and be fully aware of why digital marketing is important and how it can help them reach their goals more than anything else. Marketers need to get out of the comfort zone of traditional marketing that they have been living in for so long. They need to forget about the statements like, "I don't need a website," and "I don't need social media." All of this made sense a few years ago when running a business was largely dependent on word of mouth, reputation amongst social groups, and traditional forms of marketing.

One of the concepts of traditional marketing that work is that the marketing needs to be done where most of the population or users are. By that very same concept, in the modern day and age, most of the population and users are on the internet more than anywhere else. This means that as the users and target audience are switching over to the digital realm, you need to make the switch with them as well in order to retain them and gain new audiences. Digital marketing is the new traditional marketing for the new generation. Small business owners need to know why it is important to take quality pictures, use reviews on websites, feature fresh content, and optimize their platforms to rank high on search engines. They need to know that the Internet is capable of giving them more information than any other form of marketing has given before.

The audience for this book should not be limited to just small business owners looking to grow their businesses. I wanted a book that would be able to communicate everything I have learned and experienced so far in understandable terms to anyone and everyone who wants to start following the trends of digital marketing and get better at it. This audience may not necessarily be tech savvy, or even marketing savvy, but has an interest in, gaining an advantage through the use and adoption of new marketing techniques. One of the core motives behind writing this book is that I have seen digital marketing has become increasingly popular in a much shorter span of time than traditional marketing. In fact, digital marketing is still growing at an exponential rate. You would be surprised to see the numbers or figures that large companies are investing in digital marketing. The reason is that the results that digital marketers have been able to achieve are widespread and effective.

This book will go through every aspect of digital marketing and make it crystal clear with lots of DIY ideas and directions on how to choose the right strategy, or hire the right agency. At the end of this volume, you will have accumulated experiences to apply to your business and make it grow in ways you did not imagine possible. The best thing is that I have tried and tested each of these tactics on my own business before deciding to share it with other small business owners.

What Will You Learn from This Book?

        The main aim of this book is to teach you how to build and sustain your business as a brand with a dominating social media presence, as per the requirements of the modern world with the onset of modern online technology. To piece together all the puzzle of digital marketing and connect all of the dots of online marketing, which will lead to the lucrative growth of your business. However, that alone is a vast process so if I were to classify it under smaller learning portions or steps, they would be:

- How to market your business on various digital platforms
- How to deal with digital marketing as you run your business and adopt new marketing techniques
- How to track marketing efforts that you are conducting in the online world
- Grow your business in a way that can be sustained in the oncoming digital era and be successful at it
- Use of the cloud software CRM (Clients Relationship management) to grow and be able to value your business, perhaps for an exit strategy.

        The next chapter will delve into what digital marketing is. So before we proceed to the actual implications and dealings, you'll have a clear-cut idea of what fields you are going to be operating in. After that, we will go through why building an online presence is important and how it can be done. We will detail how to use SEO, building traffic via organic channels, managing an online reputation, and making efficient use of paid advertising. We'll also cover social media marketing and the implications that has for you as a business owner. Also covered in this text is the topic of email marketing and how it has already become a replacement for one form of traditional marketing, as well as CRM marketing, lead funnel and conversions. Then we will take a look at offline marketing as well.

        Following this pattern, by the time we reach the end of the book, you will have become familiar with all of the above-mentioned objectives and will be in a better position to grow your business by using these methods.

Chapter 2

What is Digital Marketing

Assets

- The company website
- Blog posts
- E-Books and whitepapers
- Infographics
- Interactive tools
- Social media channels
- Earned online coverage
- Online brochures
- Branding assets

Tactics

Search Engine Optimization (SEO):
This is the process of making your website optimized in a manner that it shows up higher in the search engine results and thus increases the amount of traffic that your website gets.

Content Marketing:
This involves two things; the creation of content about your products, services or brand and the promotion of that content to generate brand awareness, increase traffic growth and customers.

Inbound Marketing:
This type of marketing uses the assets of digital marketing and the theory of push and pull marketing. In inbound marketing, online content is used to attract target customers onto a certain website, or rather; it focuses on pulling customers instead of pushing a message.

Social media marketing:
This refers to the efforts made to promote your brand or portfolio or even your content on social media platforms. The aim is to increase brand awareness, divert traffic to other places and generate a following that can boost your customer base. It is done through the following ways:

 Pay per click (PPC)

 **Marketing Automation**

 Affiliate Marketing

 Email Marketing

 **Native Advertising**

 Online Public Relations (PR)

11

The previous chapter should have given you a good idea of what the motives behind this book are and what fields of work I operate in. Since most of my life is dedicated to digital marketing, one of the motives is to explain in detail the ins and outs of digital marketing along with everything else related to it. The reason for this is that I believe digital marketing is something that is going to be more common for the upcoming generations than the traditional type of marketing that we have known for so long. Even in our present day and age, digital marketing has risen to the top-- surpassing all other promotional activities in a relatively short time. This is because the results have been widespread and very effective. Since I am an insider on this, I've also had a look at behind the scenes of what is going on. Those of us insiders know the importance of learning more about digital marketing.

In this chapter, we will go through what digital marketing is in a nutshell. We will look at the definition and then break it down to see how each part of the process is applied or used. Next, we will look at the basic tools used in digital marketing, namely SEO (search engine optimization), social media, and Google Ads (formerly AdWords) since all of these are commonly used in the world's leading agencies. Without further ado, let's start with the concept and definition of digital marketing.

Digital Marketing

Before we get into what digital marketing is and what it does, let's have a look at its history first. This term is not that old. It was coined in the 1990s as people began to switch to different channels of marketing when the mainstream channels started to get saturated. Then in 2000, a survey conducted in the United Kingdom found that the majority of retailers did not have their domain addresses registered. So from 2000 to 2010, when the world was introduced to devices and gadgets that were capable of using and accessing digital media, there was a sudden growth in online media channels being used for marketing. There was a sudden shift in the lifestyle and trends of individuals as people started to spend double the time on the Internet than they spent previously. There was a time period when you might have heard that the way people shop and buy or even browse had changed or that it had become easier to shop online. After experiencing this sudden boom, data collected in 2012 and 2013 showed that the growth was still going strong and it hinted that this was the beginning. This means that the growth was probably going to be exponential as more media channels opened up. At that time, the term digital marketing was known by other terms in different regions. For example, in the U.S.A. it was known as online marketing whereas in Italy it was known as web marketing. After 2013, the term digital marketing was started to be used world-wide as a common term.

Digital marketing is an umbrella term used to describe an organization's online marketing efforts. Organizations and firms use digital channels such as the Google search engine, email, social media sites, and websites to connect with and build a customer base by finding relevant prospective customers. The purpose of marketing has always been to connect and remain connected with your existing audience at the right place and right time while also looking for opportunities to expand the customer base. One of the things any firm does to accomplish this is be where the audience is. In previous times, this meant

13

that firm representatives had to be on the field all the time and visit physical sites where the customers would generally be. With the onset of technology, this means that now most of the audience is spending time on the Internet-- and that is where you need to be. This created a way for digital marketing to enter the scene.

To put digital marketing in a definition, it is the advertising activities and promotion efforts of products or services that are delivered through online or digital channels like email, social media, apps etc. The difference from traditional marketing is that the channels in digital marketing offer the advantage to an organization to analyze the marketing campaigns in real time. This way, savvy digital marketers are able to see what is working, what is not, and what kind of effect it is having on the masses.

To do this, a number of things are monitored by digital marketers. Metrics of what is being viewed, how often is it viewed, how long it is viewed for; what content works, what locations do audiences prefer, where do sales conversions occur. One must also learn about the dynamics of your niche audience groups that are targeted or are using the products or services.

Digital marketing also makes use of text messaging, instant messaging, cell phone apps, podcasts, electronic billboards, digital televisions, and radio channels. As an organization that engages in digital marketing, everything from our website to online branding assets is valuable as a resource for digital marketing. On this range of online channels, it is easy to classify everything into two fields: assets and tactics, because that is the way digital marketers tend to use them. Digital marketers that have a good grip on these have a clear idea of how to use and apply each asset or tactic to get closer to the company's goals.

Assets

These are the resources available to you to utilize in your marketing efforts.

- **The company website**
- **Blog posts**
- **E-Books and whitepapers**
- **Infographics**
- **Interactive tools**
- **Social media channels** (Facebook, LinkedIn, Reddit, Twitter, Instagram etc.)
- **Earned online coverage** (public relations, social media, and reviews)
- **Online brochures**
- **Videos**
- **Branding assets** (logos, taglines, graphics, and fonts)

Tactics

- **Search Engine Optimization (SEO):** This is the process of making your website optimized in a manner that it shows up higher in the search engine results and thus increases the amount of traffic that your website gets.

- **Content Marketing:** This involves two things; the

creation of content about your products, services or brand and the promotion of that content to generate brand awareness, increase traffic growth and customers.

- **Inbound Marketing:** This type of marketing uses the assets of digital marketing and the theory of push and pull marketing. In inbound marketing, online content is used to attract target customers onto a certain website, or rather; it focuses on pulling customers instead of pushing a message.

- **Social media marketing:** This refers to the efforts made to promote your brand or portfolio or even your content on social media platforms. The aim is to increase brand awareness, divert traffic to other places and generate a following that can boost your customer base. It is done through the following ways:

- **Pay per click (PPC):** In this method, traffic is diverted to your website every time an ad is clicked because you have paid a publisher to do so. Google Ads is the most common type of PPC service.

- **Affiliate Marketing:** This type of marketing functions on a commission system so it is performance-based. Participants who generate sales, leads, or traffic to their partner receive a commission for marketing your products or services on your website.

- **Native Advertising:** Native advertising usually refers to advertisements that are focused on the content or open with the content and are present on a platform simultaneously with other content that is non-paid. For example, posts that are sponsored by BuzzFeed are one way to do this but some groups of people also include social media posts as a part of this advertising.

- **Marketing Automation:** Since many actions of marketing have to be repeated continuously such as email, social media, and various website actions-- it is better to have these tasks automated. Thus, marketing automation refers to the software that exists to automate these marketing processes.

- **Email Marketing:** A lot of companies use emails to market their products and services or to communicate with their customers. Through emails, content is usually promoted and discounts and events are made known to divert people toward the company website.

- **Online Public Relations (PR):** It is similar to traditional PR building. The only difference is that this occurs in the online space. So digital marketers will aim to secure earned online coverage with online publications, blogs, and other content-based activities.

Why Is Digital Marketing So Important?

In the beginning of this chapter, I explained the history of digital marketing and the changes it brought with it. Digital media has become so prevalent in our society that anybody can have access to loads of information at any time and any place they want. It is becoming an increasing source of many things, including but not limited to: news, entertainment, shopping, social interaction, etc. Before such technology was available to us, marketing communication consisted of you messaging your customers the details of your products or services. This message would only contain what you wanted them to know. Things are different now. Firstly, marketing itself is based primarily on the interaction between sellers and buyers-- and even buyers amongst themselves. Through the power of digital marketing, consumers are now aware of not just what buyers tell them or what a company says about its brand but also what other people are saying about the product or brand.

Any interaction that occurs among friends, relatives, peers, or even fellow consumers about a brand is primarily important. This is because people are more likely to believe those interactions than the company itself. By getting a second opinion, consumers place a higher value on brands they can trust or brands that are credible. The onset of digital media has given the consumer a power they've never had: the ability to conduct research about what they want and then make decisions more knowingly than ever before.

Another thing that the onset of digital media has done is to enable better communication channels with product or service providers. This allows for brands to make themselves more tailored, relevant and personalized to consumer preferences.

Another way to look at or judge the importance of digital marketing is to think of it as something that has just begun. The past trends and statistics I mentioned earlier in the chapter show that digital marketing is still on the course of its rise, and from the looks of it, will continue to do so. The future of traditional marketing is digital marketing. Success consists of managing and controlling more types of audience interactions than just email and messages. To simplify, these can be summarized in the Five D's that a company needs to assess consumer interactions:

- **Digital Devices:** These are the devices used by customers to interact with businesses. These include anything ranging from smartphones and tablets to desktop computers, televisions, and gaming devices as well.

- **Digital Platforms:** These are the spaces that can be accessed using digital devices where the interactions can take place like Facebook, Google, and Twitter etc.

- **Digital Media:** Digital media consists of channels that are either paid, owned, or earned for reaching the consumer base and engaging them through advertising, promotions, and social networks.

- **Digital Data:** This is all the insights and statistics that companies collect from the interaction going on in online spaces. These include audience profiles and patterns of interaction, many of which are governed by law in most countries.

- **Digital Technology:** This is the technology that companies use to create the interactive experiences for audiences when they come to interact with websites and apps or even in-store kiosks.

Primary Benefits of Digital Marketing

When I took one of my first advertising and marketing communication courses, we were taught about placing an advertisement in a newspaper. It is quite difficult to find out how many people actually flipped to the page where your advert is and read it. From finding out how many newspapers were sold in the morning that day to the average number of people who would visit the section of your advert, and the type of people amongst the audience that would pay attention to it; all of this is done to find out the return on investment (ROI). Even then, these are not considered surefire ways to find out if the advert was responsible for the sales at all.

In contrast, this is where all the benefits of digital marketing come in. You can now measure your ROI in real time. Here is a classification of these benefits:

- **Website Traffic:** In traditional or offline marketing, it is very hard to find out how many people are actually interacting with your brand until someone makes contact with a salesperson or your company directly. This is similar to finding out what times on television or radio most users are available and watching and what are the peak times etc. However, now you can see the exact number of people who view your websites as they view it. You can see what device they were using, what other pages they visited, and where they came from. All of this intelligence is classified as digital analytics data, which is used to find out on which marketing channels you should spend more or less time.

- **Content Performance:** This is the same as print media creating leads for the sale of your products and services-- except the fact that previously print media had adverts, brochures, and letters, etc. But now all of these are online in the form of blogs and articles. The benefit is that you can find out how many views or hits each piece got. You can even get voluntary contact details from the people who downloaded something from a website which is a bonafide form of lead creation.

*   **Attribution Modeling:** This is when a company uses effective marketing strategies that can be used with the right tools which allow you to trace your sales back to the point where it started, or rather the customer's first digital touchpoint. This in itself is a benefit but you can also do more with this. Having the ability to trace these routes will help you to build a database from where you can identify trends about your target consumers and make the route simpler and easier for them, thereby increasing your sales.

Challenges Faced in Digital Marketing

As with anything else, digital marketing is not a complete solution to marketing. There are some issues that need to be catered to as it evolves. The only thing for sure is that digital marketing will have more users over time than it has now. This may create some new challenges, so let's have a look at some of these issues:

*   **Increasing Data Volume:** Nowadays, consumers use online platforms for everything; and the job of digital marketers includes collecting data from everywhere a customer has been and picking out the relevant details. This creates an issue because consumers leave behind a huge trail of data on digital channels. It becomes difficult to sift through all of the data, especially when it is continuously increasing.

- **The proliferation of Digital Channels:** As is the case with most users, everyone uses multiple digital channels to satisfy their online quirks. They also use a variety of devices and different devices have different specifications, interfaces, and protocols. For consumers, it is easy to have different devices for different types of interaction, but for digital marketers, things are not so easy when they have to keep track of numerous devices using numerous channels at the same time.

- **Intensifying Competition:** This is a basic rule for everything in the world that when something is introduced, the market for it eventually gets saturated and so restrictions are placed. In the case of digital marketing, numerous digital channels are free of cost, or relatively cheap. This makes them accessible to almost every business of every size possible. As a result, basically, everyone is getting on the grid, while the grid is not expanding enough to meet everyone's needs. Amongst this sea of interactions, it is very hard to get your consumer base's attention toward your own content. This translates to spending more than others to be visible and not get lost in the sea

Chapter 3

Building An Online Presence

Why do you need to build an online presence?

Now that we have discussed and gone over what digital marketing really is and what it entails, let's move forward to discussing things that are more relative to your business now. Up until now, you should have a general idea of things that you will need to do in order to move towards growing your business and building a strong brand which means that now we can actually move towards turning the wheels a little faster.

We've become familiar with factors you have to keep in mind for short term benefits, and what factors need to be focused on for long term benefits. You should also know how important it is to have the right clients and you must have an idea why it is important to brand your products instead of just selling them or pushing them out in the economy. For both these purposes, the first and foremost important task that you need to do is start building an online presence for your business, or revamp it if you already have one.

Like we talked about in the introduction of this book, it is an absolute must for your business to have an online presence, whether it is a website, an E-commerce platform, a social media page, local listing directory profile, such as Yelp page, Google my Business, a niche directory or a combination of those things. Getting your business online will lead to you reaping major benefits in the future. It doesn't matter if your company does not conduct business online, there will still be clients and potential customers expecting to find out more about your company and its credibility online. If you have no presence, that means you are losing out on the opportunity to increase your consumer base and spread the word about your business.

Here are some of the reasons at the top my head to make you see why you might want to build an online presence:

1. **Make it easier for potential customers to come to you:**
   An ocean of potential customers now exist in the digital realm and prefer to look for businesses that are already established there. Transitioning to the online world will mean that you will be making things easier, not just for a lot of existing customers, but for millions of potential customers who only need to discover you.

2. **Make it easier to showcase your products and services:**
   Unlike traditional methods where a company's products or services would be showcased at physical locations like showrooms or shops, much of it can be done now virtually, making it much easier for everyone. You can showcase your products and services through your website or social media page. This can do two things for you; spike up the interest in your business offerings; and make it less of a hassle for consumers to engage with you.

3. **Make it easier to build relationships with customers and potential customers**
   Once online, you will see that it will become easier to build relationships and sustain them because it will be easier and less costly for both of you to remain in contact with each other, share your latest product lines, or to get feedback on your products. There will not be a large amount of time delays, nor will it require trips here and there to engage with consumers.

4. **Make it easier to market your brand**
   Marketing your business and brand will also get a whole lot easier because you will have to direct your efforts to one space rather than multiple spaces.

The results will also be more effective as well because most of the audience is present online too these days.

A digital marketing agency is there to assist for this very purpose, to build your online presence in a manner that encompasses and makes use of all the features and openings available through the internet. Basically, the kind of business you are running and the opportunities it can give rise to will be combined with the opportunities available through the online world. You need to transition your business over to the digital realm and make the physical aspects of your business connect with the digital side, so that it works in cohesion. There are a number of ways that this can be achieved.

A good digital marketing agency will go over each one of them with you. Keeping that in mind, we will now go over the various methods or steps that will need to be taken to build your business's online presence.

Building a website:

All businesses, no matter how small, should have a website. The first thing you need to start focusing on is having a place for your logo, message, vision and any other information that you have in mind for you to convey to your audience about your business. This place will be your business brand website first of all because as we know, the internet is where everyone usually goes to find something. So instead of having indirect channels or sources of information about your business and your products or services, it is better to have an official source, owned by you, where customers can visit and get to know what they want from a credible and trusted source.

Your website can be extremely basic at first, but it should contain the fundamental information that customers, both existing potential, need or want. Everything that you put on your website should be updated and complete. For example, you might have experienced this a lot when visiting restaurant websites. They often times have a website that's missing their current menu, their operating hours, or contact information etc. Google will more often than not have this information, but their website will not. Obviously, this becomes frustrating, and my choice of where I get my food from will most likely be affected because of this. I do not want to trust a review from some other source or look at a menu from another source because it might not be updated or synced with the correct information from the restaurant. I want to know from the restaurant itself what they are offering.

Everything that you put on your website also needs to be optimized for user viewing if you want it to be successful. You will need to make sure that the tabs you put on your website are user friendly-- everything from the colors, text, and images should be geared towards optimized representation of your brand. Keep in mind that you will also need to have appealing call to actions on your website as well. Call to action refers to directing customers to interact with your website in ways such as 'view our catalog' or 'download now' or 'place order' etc.

A basic website is not very hard to set up using an application like WordPress, which is known widely as a free blogging tool, but is a very effective content management system. You can also build a fairly simple Shopify store for your e-commerce business. You also have the option of paying to get a subscription for the premium version and you can also add an online shop to your website. I am emphasizing this part because statistics showed that in 2013, seventy percent of the consumers preferred to do their shopping online. Of course, it depends on what kind of business you have, but it is always possible to integrate at least some elements for placing orders if not complete shopping on your website.

The point of your website is to have all the necessary information that your consumers and clients might potentially need or want. That experience must be as easy as possible. This step may seem very obvious at first, but for many business owners, as they start to begin this step, it suddenly becomes daunting because suddenly there are a million possibilities for website designing, themes and producing content and so on. It is important to remember at this point that your initial goal is simply to build a website and be online.

Don't fret over small aesthetic details, because its appearance and content can be made better over time. The first version of your website is not going to represent you in the digital world for eternity. In fact, all of it can be changed within seconds, unlike traditional forms of marketing like billboards and advertisements. And keep in mind, for better positioning in search engines, your website needs to be constantly updated with fresh content like blogs, upcoming and past events, galleries, case studies, new product lines, seasonal promotions, etc. From my experiences of running a digital marketing firm, I've noticed that the energy and focus spent on the initial website is too big, and after the website starts generating traffic, clients always start wanting to change the site, evolving it to their businesses and keep improving it. You should start off with a simple site and keep improving it as your online presence grows.

Identifying your branding assets:

Branding assets are all of the elements available to you that can be used to describe or portray your business and brand in a manner that sets it apart from your other competitors. Altogether, they need to create an image of your business that is unique. These can include a wide array of things, including, but not limited to, logos, fonts, colors, scheme, taglines, backgrounds, and basically anything that you can tailor or customize to be in line with your business or idea. Of course, this means that you have a lot of options available to you since you can practically combine anything you want. But in order to create a lasting impact and a dominating presence, you will have to delve deeper into branding assets and their usage. Before you choose your options, you will have to research intelligently and then make your choices.

For instance, when it comes to colors, each color signifies a meaning attached to it. Every color is linked to some sort of emotion that it provokes, like a neural pathway in the brain which leads to a certain feeling. White will signify a sense of cleanliness, red will show danger or desire, blue will bring about a calming or peaceful effect, and black might denote gloominess or mysteriousness.

In the same way that color choice works as a branding asset, the other elements like fonts or logos will have certain things attached to them as well. An italic font may come off as fancy or informal while a bold font may come off as imposing and too out there. When you start to make a mix of these elements, be sure to know what effect each of them brings about and what effect you want to be brought about in your consumer. Also, when mixing and matching elements, the effect that one element may have on it's own will be gone, and you will have to look at the combined effect. Doing this may be time consuming, but it has to be done right because these are some of the first things that your target audience will see and notice. A lot of these effects are brought about in their minds without them being even consciously aware about it. You should also keep in mind the relevance of any element you choose with your brand, don't get lost in the elements themselves that you forget that they need to be aligned with your business goals. It is best if the elements add up harmoniously to match with the brand and business-- the trick isn't just in making it look attractive.

The reason why branding assets should be focused on here is because first of all they will be on your website and secondly because they will be in other places online. As part of your online presence, these are going to be a vital part: based on the psychology of customers. When a client visits your website, they should be able to read all the content that there is, and then relate to the branding assets you are using. They may also never get a chance to visit your website and instead hear about your business from somewhere else.

Considering that, your branding assets will be used in other places apart from your website as well. From the packaging of your products, the letterheads of your company to the advertisements placed anywhere, all of it will contain them in one manner or the other. When a client or consumer notices your logo or anything else related to your company, or even a product need that is related to what you offer, they go through a mental process recalls all businesses that could fill the need. Similarly, when they see one of your branding assets in a search or for, it is going to provoke an image of your business in their minds.

What you do with your branding assets decides what kind of image comes to their mind. You have to account for the fact that not everyone is going to visit your website, but a number of consumers might just come across your logos, offers, and advertisements online in other spaces or forums. Sometimes, these assets may even be the deciding factor whether they visit your website or not.

Managing social media accounts:

Once you are done with your website, you can now focus on diversifying your digital presence in social media. Social media is an important part of your online presence that improves your chances of generating additional revenue and building lasting customer loyalty. It allows customers, potential customers and other interested parties to engage easily via a channel that plays an important role in their everyday lives.

There are multiple channels you can use to divert traffic to your website or promote your brand. Nowadays people appreciate it if brands have social media accounts that are consistently updated and maintained because it becomes easier for them if everything is showing up on their feeds rather than going to a website to check it. Having a business profile on every social account that is relevant will help you connect with more people, including a wider variety of demographics as well. Plus, once you start keeping a social media account, the messages and content you share on them will start to become more creative as you will tailor it for that account only.

Although not every social media channel will be relevant to each business, it's definitely worth looking into your options. For example, Facebook and Instagram will serve a purpose for almost any business –they are great platforms to post news, tips, photos, and videos, and answer questions. After getting the two important accounts going, you might also find Twitter, Snapchat, LinkedIn, YouTube, Pinterest, Tumblr, Foursquare helpful. It is up to you to try out for yourself which channels are better suited for your business.

Instagram, for example is a photo sharing network, so it will work better for businesses that rely on photos. Those businesses who need to focus on aesthetic beauty to drive interest should make use of Instagram. It's important to consider your target demographic – Instagram has around one-hundred thirty to one-hundred fifty million users in the USA, over two-thirds of which are women between the ages of 18 and 45. With Instagram, you'll also need to keep a smartphone handy to properly access your account and engage with your audience.

Once you've decided which social media channels to use, get a clear idea of the kind of content you can share. The more compelling and engaging your material is, the more likely your followers will like, comment and share your posts. Engagement is key to promoting your brand – not only will it make you more appealing to existing customers, but the more interaction that goes on, the higher the chance is that their friends will be exposed to your brand. After all, many times friends are monitoring what their friends are doing on social media-- and they may become intrigued by what you have to offer.

Local & Niche Directories

Before the internet boom, it was very important to the growth of a business to be listed in Thomas Book and Yellow Pages, as well as local newspapers and classified Ads. Nowadays those traditional channels migrated online, such as Google My Business, Yelp, Yp.com, local chambers of commerce, Home Advisor, Trip Advisor, etc.

It's very important for your business to be listed on such directories, since those are the channels where potential clients are searching to conduct business with. Most of them offer free listings, while some of them require minimum membership and most of them offer paid marketing for improving your listing visibility in their database. Sometimes business owners wonder, how come my business is listed on Google or Yelp. I've never signed up for it. Based on US Law, section 230 Communication Decency Act, generally protects online platforms from liability for content posted by third parties, such as users of their software/platform. This means your Yelp listing was created by Yelpers: your customers. You have an option to claim the listing and take partial control of it, but you can not delete it, since it was generated by a third party. You can claim on Yelp that you are out of business, which the platform will verify with their own users in order to confirm and leave the permanent mark on Yelp. I would rather suggest you claim the listings, fix it, upload your images, and add content. Keep generating good feedback from your clients.

There are also many niche directories, such as Trip Advisor for people they are travelling, or Air B&B for home owners renting out their properties, or Home Advisor for people in construction and home improvement business. Every business model type has some kind of niche directories, or forums published online-- and your business should be listed on it. Which It will not only help you grow your revenue, it will also improve your organic rankings in search engines placements.

Developing a branding ecosystem:

The last thing to do for building a strong online presence is to bring all of your brand's presence online together in line with each other. An ecosystem is made up of all of your brand's elements, all of the events revolving around your brand, along with the stories that keep fueling your brand image. Your website will sit at the core of this ecosystem and from there your presence will fan out on other social media accounts. Just like any other ecosystem, to make it sustainable you will have to keep live and transient.

Red Bull is a good example of a brand that keeps its ecosystem constantly refueled with new stories, challenges, content, events and records. If your ecosystem is functional without any clashes, then a lot of people will automatically be drawn to it and will become a part of it. A digital ecosystem consists of digital devices, your media presence on them and the interaction between consumers and your brand through these channels. If you lay out an ecosystem through these channels, then you can develop the ability to establish brand loyalty among your customers by delivering added value.

The key to keeping your online presence together after you have started building it and once you are done building it is to make sure that everything is aligned with each other. You cannot have your website promoting something different than your social media pages. The same way you cannot have your brand elements shouting something else and your company's mission or vision statement saying something else. When there is synergy across all of your online media spaces, your presence will automatically start getting stronger. You will be able to understand this better in the next chapter where will look at the mechanics of how this happens through search engine optimization, and why using it can take you further along in accelerating the growth of your business.

Chapter 4

SEO and SERP

Now that we have discussed extensively why building an online presence is going to be of utmost importance in the growth of your business. The next step is to look at one of the most important aspects of being able to do so. Search engine optimization (SEO) and search engine results pages (SERP) are the two aspects of digital marketing that have their claws wrapped around the whole digital world. Some might even go as far as to say that fifty percent of digital marketing is actually just learning the ins and outs of SEO and SERP.

So in this chapter, this is exactly what we will do. We will take a walk through the world of SEO and SERP, we will learn the basics and the functions of both of these techniques, and then examine the benefits that they can bring to a business in the digital world. After doing all of this, we will then begin to look at how these techniques can be effectively implemented in a business to start reaping those benefits.

What is SEO?

Search engine optimization is essentially one of the more recent marketing strategies that has caught on to users faster than any other tactic before it. The SEO technique basically focuses on increasing visibility through organic or non-paid results by search engines. This means that SEO includes technical and creative aspects, both of which are required to improve one's rankings, drive traffic, and increase familiarity and awareness amongst different search engines. The number one search engine in the entire world is Google, which has 70% search share on desktops and 90% search share on mobile devices. Other search engines are Yahoo, Bing, Yelp, Amazon, Apple App Store, Google Play Store etc. Any online platform, where users are able to search for results is considered a search engine. There is nothing out of the ordinary or mystical about SEO methods, as sometimes suggested by the way it is described. In fact, it is simply a measurable and repeatable process based on how search engines work, so that relevant signals can be sent to search engines. All these signals do is tell those search engines that your website pages and directory listings are worth showing in their index. How Google ranks these signals and your website pages is another procedure which we will discuss.

Of course, if you are going to be using a process that is going to send signals to search engines, then there are going to be a lot of aspects to it. This starts with the words on your page and the way that other sites are linked to your pages on the Internet. At times, all that SEO might be doing for you is making sure that the way your website is structured is in a format that makes it easier for search engines to comprehend and classify. You see, search engines look at two broad aspects of your website and content: on-site and off-site. The on-site aspect for example, is either going to be the content and things that are present on your own website, while off-site will cover the information or content that is out there about your site on other pages or elsewhere.

However, SEO is not just about building websites in a way that they become search engine friendly-- it has to deliver a good user experience. Both of these things go hand in hand.

Search engines work in a fairly simple manner. They apply formulas to analyze a large amount of data in order to determine which web pages come up first when a user searches for a certain keyword. This data that is being analyzed by the search engines is basically all of the web pages that they can find about a certain topic, or linked to a certain topic, so it will include both on site and off site content.

Google, for example, uses complex algorithms while going through this data, then it gives a score or rating to each of the websites that it has gone through along with every search that users perform on Google. So at this point we have all of the relevant websites ranked by the algorithms, and we have all of the searches ranked as well. This gives Google the ability to rank what is best in a given order for whatever search that might be performed. Now, when the algorithm is functioning, it takes a lot of factors into account when ranking and rating items and pages so that the process is as fair and trustworthy as possible. Google will look at the quality of your site, the amount of sites and pages that link your site, the amount of pages that mention your site and how many sources and users trust you and so on. There are going to be a lot of factors and in the end a cumulative score of all the factors or categories is going to be taken.

Your job here is to take a look at your target audience, and your competition, and then go through the whole process that search engines perform in reverse so that you can see what they want to see to rank you higher, step by step. Once you do this, you can start ensuring that all data and content you have on your own website and your links is in the right place and in the right order. Here you will also have to take care of the balance between on site and off site content. It is actually simple once you get the hang of it because there is not more to it than just getting the hang of how things are done.

So now that you know how Google's algorithm works, you know that one of your jobs is to come across higher in the rankings on the factors that are used to se-

38

cure your scores. You can improve your search engine rankings by improving the quality of your content on your site. In a similar manner, you can also affect it by gaining authority and trust amongst your audiences so that even the off site content speaks of you in a trustworthy manner. This will give you a higher score in terms of trustability for the searches that people are looking for.

Basically, there are a lot of factors that are used to give you scores, and the higher you score in each of those categories, the higher your overall score is going to be. You just have to figure out a way to improve yourself in all of these categories until your overall score starts to rise enough for the search engine to rank you higher than other competitors. This may sound a little dreary, but it is in fact making you forcibly fine tune every aspect of your website and related inbound links. It is also constantly putting you under pressure to keep coming up with better versions and better fixes. Therefore, it's best that no area or aspect of your site and its content is left untouched or ignored. Recognize the fact that there are hundreds of areas and categories that are used to give you scores. This literally means you have hundreds of opportunities to tweak your scores and get a better ranking overall.

To understand the ranking system even better, and to excel in it, think of the cumulative overall score as a weighted average, because not all categories are assigned the same importance. Some are worth more than the others, so the three most important categories that you need to be aware of are quality, trust, and authority. When it comes to quality, Google is trying to gauge is what sites are offering something valuable and unique to the searchers. It doesn't matter as much that your product is actually very different and better than your competitors, unless the content that you are using to describe them is not the same as the rest of the competition. Google will have no way of telling that your offering is different and unique unless the content is unique as well. Your task here is to show Google that your site has content that is better and different than the other sites falling under the same categories and similar search queries.

Next we come to trust. Google is going to take this very seriously because it does not want to show any deceptive sites among its search results. It wants to show those sources that are trustworthy and credible--this is how they protect their credibility. The catch here is that Google also cancels out or penalizes those sites, stores, and companies that have had bad reviews consistently. Over time, Google is going to remove them from searches. The best way to go about showing to Google that you are trustworthy is by making sure you have useful and genuine reviews. Make sure that the websites linked to you have good reviews as well and are credible sources. Make sure that you get high authoritative sites to link themselves to you. Always monitor that your audiences are happy and your partners are praising you.

Finally, we have the third most important category used to rank your site: authority. Google needs to see that you have a considerable amount of authority in your department, and the kind of information, product or service that you are selling. Why? Because Google wants to show to its users the most popular sites for their searches. If someone is looking for cars then Google will want to show the most popular car dealer to its user or searcher. Therefore, your aim becomes to show Google that you are the most popular in the kind of product of service that you deal in. You will have to start building a fan base without limits. Get as many people to like you in whatever way you can. Get people to share your content, post it on relevant pages and profiles, talk about it on platforms and blogs, leave comments and testimonials, show pictures of your products or services being used. Most importantly, keep talking and interacting with your fan base.

What is SERP?

Search engine results pages (SERP) are the complementary elements for SEO. When a user searches for something on the Internet, they are shown a number of web pages relevant to the user's search query. These queries are more often than not specific terms of phrases. The web pages that are served to these users upon searching for something are known as SERP. This may sound fairly simple to you but the thing is that every SERP is going to be unique due to the fact that every search engine, be it Google, Yahoo, and Bing all customize the results every time. Even if the search query that is used is the same and is performed on the same search engine again, the SERP will still be different even if they may look similar, they are bound to have minor differences. These differences occur because of two reasons. Firstly, it is because every search engine now tries to customize the search experience for the user by showing results that are based on a number of different factors that it takes into account. These factors include things like the location of the user, the browsing history, the search history and social settings etc. Secondly, the search engine results ages are also always changing because these search engines themselves are also constantly changing and trying out new experiments and technology to give their users a more tailored and intuitive response.

So basically, the SERPs always have content that can be classified in two kinds, organic results and paid results. Out of these two kinds, we are interested in the organic ones, we being the ones indulging in

SEO practices. If you remember, in the SEO section I described that the SEO process focuses on the organic or non-paid search engine visibility. The reason why search engine result pages are so important is because each SERP is unique and SEO professionals specialize and compete in fine tuning the content and websites themselves in a way that is able to get them higher ranking in organic search results.

On a SERP, not everything is going to be organic. Even though everything is considered a feature of the SERP, it is important to know what is what. How much of the SERP is organic depends on the nature of the search query. There are three basic types of internet searches: the informational search, the navigational search, and the transactional search.

Informational searches are those that are performed to find relevant information about a certain topic or subject. In these types of searches, the search engine does not bring out and place a lot of advertisements or any other type of paid results on the SERP because informational searches are not anything else other than just information. There users are not looking to buy something so there is no point in trying to sell. Navigational searches, on the other hand are performed when the users want to get to a specific website through their search. This includes locating websites who's URL has been forgotten or maybe when users don't exactly know the specifics. Lastly, the transactional searches are the ones that have the most commercial intent. These are the type of searches whose SERPs will have the most paid content showing up because the searches have keywords that relate to buying behavior.

It is really very important to be on the first page of the SERPs which is why SEO practitioners know how to use SERPs even if it seems monotonous. The mathematics and statistics behind this show that when the results are ranked, the 11th till the 20th results will get less than half the clicks as compared to the 1st till the 10th results. In fact, if you pause to think about it, most of us only look at the first result a lot of times. Statistics show that 90 percent of the world's population does this.

What does this mean then? In simple terms, it means that if you are ranked and shown as the second search result on a SERP, you are losing out on 90 percent of your target market instantly. This in turn means that you are losing out on many potential customers, losing out on sales, and losing out on profits. It has now become obvious why it has become a need to be on the first result in a SERP.

Benefits:

Up till now, we have looked at what is SEO and SERP is on paper and how the whole process works from both ends. All of that is useful and necessary, but sometimes going in too deep in the mechanics of it makes you lose sight of the real advantages you can reap over time. The whole point of SEO and SERP was to realize the benefits that could grow your business over time, so let's take a look at the core advantages.

The first and foremost benefit that you will be able to receive is increased traffic on your website. As we discussed earlier, the topmost pages that show up on a search engine results page receive more than double the amount of clicks. So the higher you go up in these rankings, you will see a more significant increase in the traffic. Another thing to note is that SEO also focuses on creating relevant keywords and tags as a description to show up on the results page with your website. This helps increase the click through rate and the quality of traffic.

Another way to look at SEO practices, in a

way that we have not looked at so far is that SEO is one of the most cost-effective marketing strategies. Due to the advancement in technology on the Internet, only the users who are actively looking for your offerings, even in real time, are the ones who are targeted without wasting resources elsewhere. This type of SEO helps save money when compared to outbound strategies. The leads generated by other strategies like cold calling and house calls, cost more than the leads generated by SEO.

It is also much easier to calculate and keep a track of the return on investment (ROI) or your business when using SEO thanks to the trackable and quantifiable nature of the SEO process. With SEO techniques, you can literally track and measure every part and aspect of the strategy right down to the keywords a customer might have used and the path taken to get to your site. Increase in rankings, conversions, demographic information for customers and time based purchases, everything is measurable and can be analyzed easily.

While SEO does focus on making your website become easier to navigate for search engines and their algorithms, it also focuses on making your website internally navigable as well. The structuring of the sections, the links and the content is all placed to increase the site's usability. Site usability is one of the keys to get more users and SEO does just that-- it makes it easier to find information on the website for the users while also making it easier for search engines as well.

Other types of SEOs
SEO for Amazon Store & Product Listings

Just as Google, Amazon also evolved in a search engine itself. As of today we are all aware that Amazon is the number one e-commerce platform on the market. It's helped several brands reach out to the public to buy their products. Amazon is also a complementary platform for emerging ecommerce websites that don't have enough brand awareness and weight in their industry to sell products by themselves. In fact, many brands that did not keep up with Amazon trend ran out of business, since they were relying only on traditional e-commerce business and did not generate enough revenues to survive. Amazon SEO algorithm is very different than Google, but the principles are the same. Amazon wants to show on the first page of search product results that fit users search inquiries best.

In order to improve your Amazon listing, the main fact a marketer needs to focus on is quality content. Yes, just like in your classic SEO strategy. You need to apply a very similar strategy to each product you list on Amazon. The title of your listing needs to have an adequate keyword to the product you're selling, the description of the product needs to be comprehensive and useful enough to fulfill a prospect's expectations as much as possible and you need to add as many original photos as possible. The more accurate, useful and user friendly the listing, the better its chances to rank on Amazon.

Despite the similarities with traditional SEO, Amazon Store and product listing optimization has its own particularities. Amazon was not conceived as a search engine: it's a buying platform that developed in such a way that generated the need of its own search engine within. A9 is the name of the search algorithm developed by Amazon for this purpose. Unlike traditional search engines, Amazon users are closer to the point of purchase. So the objective of A9 is to make changes according to what makes shoppers buy more frequently. It is not necessarily about what informs best but what makes the deal close better and more frequently. That's why, in the first instance, products need to improve their visibility by having the optimization we specified lines above.

The product title is the foundation of Amazon SEO strategy as it is what populates first when a user types in the search bar for a product. Your product title needs to have information like brand, product line, material, color, size, type of product, packaging and any other relevant characteristics. How you order this information along with target keywords will be determinant for your strategy. This is quite a challenge if we consider titles in organic results are usually 115-144 characters long and titles in right rail ads are 30-33 characters. Mobile titles are 55-63 characters long approximately. So placing the keywords first is essential.

SEO for Mobile Apps and ASO
(App Store Optimization)

The advent of mobile era and the subsequent Google's mobile-first update resulted in mobile apps to feature as organic search results on SERPs. If they are relevant and fulfill a query's need, mobile apps are ranked, whether users eventually install them or not. The main difference of these organic app listings is that they can be shown as an install button, so users can install them directly from search engines. Another particularity is that app links leads directly to the app the user intends to install instead of a website's landing page or homepage. This makes special sense on popular platforms like Facebook, Twitter or Yelp, where people first intend to download the app. Considering that more searches are made on mobile devices than desktop, and the rise of mobile apps market, an SEO for Mobile Apps and ASO (App Store Optimization) are the next step in the evolution of this particular market on the internet.

One particularity of this type of search engine optimization is that most of the time the name of your app becomes a keyword itself. That's why it is advisable to name your app in a way that resembles or directly refers to the product or service you're offering. This would generate a branded keyword you will be ranking for. When you do keyword research for Mobile Apps, you should describe your app and match your prospects needs. Another factor to keep in mind is App indexing, which helps a marketer to make sure his or her app is visible on search engines. In fact Google affirmed in 2015 that App indexing would be a ranking signal for Android users. App indexing also enhances an app listing with the install button we mentioned before.

You can optimize your app for a search engine or for the store you place it in. That's why you also need App Store Optimization. ASO is the process of making your app rank high on app stores rankings. To do this, you need to research and implement the right app store keywords. Some of the most popular tools for keyword research for app stores are Keyword Suggestions, Übersuggest and OneLook Reverse Dictionary. You would use those keywords to use in the name of your app, title and description of your app's ad as well as tags. It is practically mandatory to use images of your app in order to give prospects the right idea of what your app is about. A preview videos is also extremely helpful in these cases.

App stores allow users to leave reviews so paying attention to them, replying good or bad reviews and get a continuing flow of reviews in your app store greatly contributes to App Store Optimization.

SEO for Local directories
(Yelp, GMB)

The massification of high speed internet has led users to a level of active participation like never before. In recent years, review websites have become popular to the point of being possibly determinantal at the moment of making a purchase decision. This works particularly well when it comes to local businesses that provides services or live experiences such as restaurants, event venues, physical activities, and so on. Google My Business, Yelp, Yellow pages, Local.com, Manta, BBB or Angie's List are some of the hundreds of directories that arose on the internet in recent years. Just like any other activity involving search on the internet, SEO is also applied to these local directories. Their listings sometimes are counted by the millions so competition for the first places in search results are tough.

The first thing to do at the moment of performing SEO for local directories is to determine which ones of those directories suit your business niche better. There are major directories that shouldn't be ignored by any business (like GMB, Yelp, Facebook) but it is a good strategy to focus on more specific platforms depending on your industry and focus audience. This can be an exhausting task, as there are basically thousands of options available, but it's worth taking the time to do it either manually or through some sort of automatization software.

In SEO for local directories, you would need to implement keywords, photos, and relevant content just like in any other regular SEO strategy. It is recommended to add these keywords at the beginning of the business description and right next to the business name. Some other times, the business name contains a keyword that is related to the activity they develop or the products they sell.

Each listing should feature as much relevant information as possible like contact number, address, business hours and everything that makes users experience swift and fast. Just as you would do in a blog or product page on a website, it is fundamental to add a listing to the correspondent categories (maximum three).

User's reviews are a key factor in SEO for Local directories. These can be acquired in time but also encouraged in genuine ways by marketers. When it comes to client's feedback, even though five star reviews help they are not determinant. Even businesses with some one star reviews can rank well if reviews are handled strategically whether they are positive or negative. Some of these platforms, like Yelp, also offer paid options to promote your business.

Lastly, the thing that all businesses need for strong growth: brand awareness. All of this SEO and SERP processes, if done right, add to your brand awareness greatly. The use of keywords and tags make the users associate those keywords with your brand. Top position rankings on search results also make your website more trustworthy for users. All of this added together adds to the perception of your site and consequently increases brand awareness.

Chapter 5

Online Reputation Management

A few principles for online reputation management

1. Search results are algorithmically generated

2. Popularity over accuracy

3. Do not click on the repetitive pages

4. Do not engage with detractors online.

5. Use the social media when you can

6. Get your story out there

7. Protect your privacy

8. Live under the assumption that everything lasts forever

The next step after learning to utilize SEO, SERP and Digital Marketing in general, is to look at the next block in the chain that is aligned with these two tools. The next step in the process of growing your business is that you take a look at your business' website and start managing its reputation, or building one if you feel that there is potential to do so.

I think there is almost always a potential to build your reputation. The process of managing reputation also entails or building it up. If you think about it, managing your reputation means that you are actively keeping it in a certain shape and the longer it stays in that shape, it is automatically also enhancing your reputation since one of the factors that counts is for how long a company maintains a solid reputation. For example, when a company has a reputation for taking care of its customers and there has not been a mishap since the last ten years; or a company is reputed to be always coming with better incentives for its employees. Both of these examples include managing and building a reputation over time which is what this chapter is going to focus on.

The crux of this chapter will be to identify the various methods that we can use or implement to make your business website and social pages more alluring, Then, we need to make them as solid as possible. However, before we start looking at the ways through which your website or social media pages can be made more trustworthy and reputable, there are some things that you should know about online reputation management that are important for your brand or business as well as your personal self.

Why does online reputation management matter?

A reputation exists whether it is in the real

world or any other circle. This book has been focused on the online world because that is where digital marketing takes place and that is where you need to focus your reputation building efforts. How you look or are perceived online now directly affects your business and career just like it would have in the real world in previous times. Negative items or associations showing up online can do a lot of damage to your business and career, whereas having a positive reputation online will translate to having a prosperous business with a growing consumer base. The importance of building and managing your reputation in the online space lies in the following four points.

1. Literally anyone can say anything about you or your business online without getting into real trouble, whether it is true or not.

If you read the statement again you will be able to see that it has a lot of potential for a lot of possibilities to happen. If you ever manage to upset anyone through your business then that means that you have actively created an opening for them to go online and trash your business. However, if you manage to upset or offend anyone on even a personal level without having any sort of link to your business, it still means the same thing. If they know who you are or find out who you are and that you run a business-- they can just as easily go and write a bad review somewhere or trash talk about your business. For example you might end up offending a neighbor because their dog annoys you or because they leave the trash out on the sidewalk. There is nothing stopping that neighbor to go and start writing an article or bad review about your business online. They can use a false name and you might never know who it was and even if they do not do that there are still no laws in place to protect you or stop him or her from doing it.

I once knew an owner of a laundromat business who rubbed off on the wrong side of a teenager who was living alone and trying to do her laundry right when the shop was closing. The teenager did not like the fact that the laundromat owner did not let her do her load of clothes and let the shop remain open for a little later than usual. Even though the laundromat owner is usually flexible and does not mind doing little favors like these he had to go visit a sick relative, so he refused. The teenager then went online and started giving out bad yelp reviews about the laundromat and it took some time for the owner to track down where the reviews were being made from and then check out who lived there. What I am trying to say here is that it may not even be your fault at times but you have to be careful and not rule out the possibility that this can happen. It can literally be anyone: an ex, a fired employee, or even someone you received a promotion over.

2. People are always going to be looking you up online and make decisions based on what they are able to find.

This is something that we already established in the first chapter, the fact that people are moving increasingly towards the online realm, which means that over time more and more people are going to be online to find out what they can about you if they are interested you or your offerings. The problem here is that it is not going to be completely in your control what shows up on the Internet about you, so when people look you up on the internet and find stuff related to you it is not always going to be what you want or what you have put up yourself.

Every day, over one billion names are searched on the Internet through Google. This is also a two-pronged process because it does not matter if your business has a good reputation online whereas your own personal reputation online is not in synchronization. That will make the people looking at these things doubt the reputation of your business as well because they might think that it has been faked. This can also happen the other way around. While you may not have ever looked yourself or your company up, it is safe to say that someone else has. And if someone has, that means that they have already making judgements based on what they were able to find. More than forty percent of the people who search online for a person on entity will make their decision whether or not to do business with them. I am sure you would not want to take that risk.

1. Everything that you do online is going to be recorded forever in the online world which means that at the end of the day you will need more tools to make sure this does not damage your reputation

With the onset of the Internet, it gradually turned in to everything being done online. We now also have the technology to track and store all of that activity without ever possibly losing it. What does this mean for you and your business? The fact that everything and anything you may have posted before a business, before undergoing a major transformation in your life or before you gave up on something, is still there somewhere and can be accessed or pulled out to the front.

That means everything we post on Facebook or Twitter and every item we search for, web-

site we visit, and online transaction exists somewhere. This extends to private information as well.
There have been cases where hackers have been
able to breach the privacy of anyone and bring various private exchanges or views under the limelight.
That makes it all the more scary because things
that may not have been public-- like private emails
or messages-- even if deleted-- can still come back.
Added to this, places online where outdated laws
that have not been kept up to match the evolving
technology pose a risk in this regard as well because
it makes it easier for people to gain access to information.

> 2. Having impeccable online content is surely
> going to help you but most people do not know
> how to do it.

The market for everything is becoming
increasingly competitive, which means that you will
have to step up your game and publish compelling
content on your website and social pages for you to
be able to draw in customers. This means an increasing amount of companies, individuals and other customers for your business will be looking for positive
information related to you.

Everyone who is in to digital marketing
knows that their content needs to be compelling and
attractive. But the problem with most people is they
really don't know how to do it. Online reputation management consists of increasing the positive footprint
of your business in every area we have discussed in
this book so far. One warning that business owners
must heed: That outsourcing the content to a writer or
constantly updating your social pages with stuff that
may not be very interesting will get you nowhere in
the long run.

A few principles for online reputation management

Over the years I have developed a few rules in this area of online reputation management. I have found that keeping them in mind generally helps you make better decisions and keep your online reputation strategies focused, even when you think it might be a difficult decision to make.

1. **Search results are algorithmically generated**
   Since we are building your reputation online, it is imperative that you know everything online is based on complex calculations and algorithms. You cannot really employ people to deal with the amount of information out there, so the process has become automated. This in turn means that all of the major search engines and social media platforms deploy algorithms to make educated guesses about what their users are looking for or might find interesting.

2. **Popularity over accuracy.**
   The main drawback that comes with this auto-mated process of algorithms is that humans can be a better judge of what information accurately reflects you.

3. **Popularity becomes one of the main measuring standards.** This is the reason why searches performed extensively during a time period or embarrassing posts, lawsuits discarded years ago are often brought up again in the limelight and could potentially dominate someone's online reputation.

4. **Do not click on the repetitive pages.**
   It's possible there are going to be negative search results pages and irrelevant sites in your

search results. But the only way to reduce them from appearing time and time again is by not clicking on them. As explained in the previous principle, popularity is one of the judging factors for algorithms and so you clicking on something will tell the search engine that it is relevant. The next time you search for something remotely linked to it, the search engine will provide it higher up in your search results.

5. **Try to avoid any sort of association or footprint with these sorts of things.** Do not tell your friends to go visit the page, especially if your social media account is connected because the search engine will automatically think what is interesting for your friends is something that you are going to be interested in as well.

6. **Do not engage with detractors online.**
Like I explained in the earlier section of this chapter when we were discussing why online reputation management is so important: you will come across people that will be trying to derail you and your business in the online space. If someone writes something unflattering about you or your business or gives you a bad review, refrain from engaging with them on the same forum and posting a comment. You do not want to bring more light to the issue and give it more weight. This could make it into something bigger than it is. You have no idea of knowing how genuine the person is or how malicious that person can be and twist your words from your response against you and your reputation.

7. **Use the social media when you can.**
Social media sites are among the first ones to go through algorithmic processing by search en-

gines. Thus, they rank well in search results. So it is a good idea to sign up on sites like Twitter and LinkedIn. Sign up using your full name instead of a different ID so that you are easier to identify, and make sure your details are up to date. The good thing about these sites is that you have the option to control the amount of privacy you want and the content that is displayed.

8. **Get your story out there**
It is a general rule that one can only really promote the materials that are out there. This means that you need to have a solid story and accurate content so that you can promote it with invested efforts. If the story is shaky or the content is flimsy it becomes hard to promote it and it becomes even harder for others to promote it or speak well about it if they cannot relate to it or do not trust it enough. The best way to gain trust and be relatable is by getting your story out there and integrating it with your business. Some people portray it to be the reason for starting their business, some people say it is why the love doing what they are doing and so on. You need to find a story that suits your business and you and then build on it. Make some things revolve around it. If it goes well you can make a side blog for it separately or even a YouTube channel.

9. **Protect your privacy.**
I know that it is in your control what you choose to share on social sites and your own website, but it is always a good idea to keep a track on them and constantly check on what privacy policies have been updated. Since it is not in your control what others dispense about you, it is also a good idea to keep tabs on the personal

identifiable information that might be out there about you. Opt out of services that sell your personal information, and remove your data from people-search sites.

10. **Live under the assumption that everything lasts forever**
This is one of the things that was included in why online reputation matters or is important for obvious reasons but it is also a principle that you will have to live by when maintaining your reputation online. You never know what can work against you because old posts and published items may come up in search results at the top because it might seem relevant to a certain situation, even if it is not. Search results are not arranged in chronological order, and anything published online has the potential to be permanently there.

What makes a website usually appealing?

The reason I put this in the last, even though I mentioned it in the beginning, is because the other stuff we've covered is much more important to know. Everything discussed before this section should be considered before you start coming up with ways to make your website and social media pages more attractive.

Another reason is that when you know all of it, you will automatically be in a better position to make your website better. In terms of design, there is an element of creativity that cannot really be taught, but only refined. If you are not a designer, then making your website visually appealing might be tough, and you might have to hire a designer for this purpose. So here is the best way to tackle the aesthetic essentials of your site.

1. **Design and color**
   A good website that can catch and retain the interest of someone visiting must have a conscious color scheme and a solid design. Every color and every combination of color brings a sort of feeling or thought in the human mind, so whatever scheme you chose has to be given thought to.

   Good design also communicates care and credibility almost instantaneously. If the design is too much or making the website difficult to maneuver, then it can shut down interest in the person visiting it.

2. **Pictures and graphics**
   Pictures with quality add to the visual appeal of the website and this is one of the easiest steps to gain an edge over your competition. Even now, a lot of websites do not have well-placed and composed pictures of their offerings, office, or teams. Take a specific look at how the website will look on phones, and see if you can make the pictures interactive or fun.

3. **Usability**
   This is one of the key features of a good website. Make things easy to understand and navigate. There is no need to come up with alternate terms for conventional names such as 'Main Lobby' instead of 'Home'. The buttons should be distinct, the dropdown menus should be smooth and simple, and the overall page layout should be focused on what is the most important topic of that page.

4. **Consistency**
   Once you have set up a design language on your

homepage, make sure that the rest of your website follows the same design language. This will result in the visitors spending less time figuring out how to adapt to the website and figure out what you are saying.

Chapter 6

Paid Advertising

Avoid Long Tail Keywords

Keep Your Tracking Ready

Create a Landing Page

Review Results Regularly

By this point, we have gone over quite a few ways to build and manage your online reputation. It should be enough to give you a start and a know-how about how marketing differs in the digital realm. Each aspect has potential benefits for the growth of businesses if applied correctly.

Digital marketing is all about being at the right place and at the right time... Even if there are time differences and geographical barriers. It is a virtual space, filled with potential clients, each of whom have moved away from traditional marketing and expect everything to be available online. Whoever is able to build a solid reputation on any platform has the potential to attract more and more traffic.

In this chapter, we are going to take things one step further. Assuming that you have been able to build your business' reputation online so far through the basic tools. Once you start getting traffic to your website, you have to have a way to sustain it and cater to it without compromising more traffic. Depending on how much you are willing to grow, it is also important to note that you will not be able to attract the same desired traffic to your website at the beginning. You will want to increase the amount of traffic once you have gotten the hang of digital marketing basics.

After SEO and SERP, the next step to attract more favorable traffic to your website is by using paid advertising. Since this advertising is paid, you can make sure that traffic is definitely diverted to your site. Otherwise, it can end up costing you more than you planned. In order to make sure that you are getting the most out of paid advertising, here are a few things you need to be careful about:

Understand What Long Tail Keywords Are and How They Work

One of the most commonly used tools for paid advertising is keywords, so the most important thing to grasp before diving in to paid advertising is to understand how keywords actually work. One problem with these types of tools is that they have the tendency to push people and make them use broader keywords to try and catch more traffic. This practice ends up being more expensive and less effective.

What you should do is to look for the keywords that customers use rather than the keywords that have the highest traffic attached to them. This means that you have to be aware of, and be on the lookout for keywords that are referred to as long tail keywords.

Long tail keywords are basically longer than the usual keywords and are also more specific. They are added to the head keywords and make up the majority of the search-driven traffic. Head keywords are the broader keywords and are less effective, but when added to another keyword to form a long tail keyword, they become more useful. For example, social media marketing is a head keyword. Social media marketing courses is a little more specific keyword but cannot be considered a long tail keyword. On the other hand, social media marketing courses online is a long tail keyword because it is not searched as frequently as social media marketing. The long tail keyword narrows things down for relevance and specifics
.

It is a very common mistake for beginners to choose the wrong keywords for their SEO or PPC because it all seems so easy. It is not a good idea to choose a head keyword because you will be spending more money while not getting enough return on your investment. To get a bang for your buck, it is advisable to target a larger number of lower traffic terms for the same amount of money that is spent on a head keyword and target only a few high traffic terms, alongside.

Another good idea to include in this strategy is to look for keywords from your own website that customers might potentially use to search for you. Once you find out what your customers are looking for, you will be able to invest your money in more specific keywords and naturally get a higher return.

Know the Territory

In the digital realm, there are a lot of places that you can buy to put advertisements, with each place having its set of weaknesses and strengths. To find out where your advertisement might be worth placing, get to know the possible and major types of paid advertising.

Display or banner ads are one of the most prominent types of ads because they stand out on any webpage. The fact that they are so noticeable and effective is that they target the customers that are not really looking for something new and are on that page for something else. A good example of this is newspaper articles online and the banner ads on them. People who visit those pages are there to read the news and do not look for something that a business might be selling. It becomes more of a hit and miss situation with your money.

Text advertisements catch your eye on a primary Google search page. These ads are generally less expensive than banner ads and target customers that are actually looking for something specific. For text advertisements to be effective, you have to combine them with good keywords. One of the places to place your paid advertisements is Google Ads (formerly Google AdWords). It is the most common choice and has the best functioning process of showing display and text ads that are highly associated with keywords. Bing and Yahoo! are similar to Google and offer an alternative platform for doing the same thing. These options might bring in less traffic but have more relevant users, which can translate to a better return on your investment.

Among social networks, Facebook, LinkedIn, and Instagram have become very popular for advertisements in the past few years. Facebook is especially developing itself more for the usage of ads. Here, the ads are not only combined with keywords, but they are also associated with the site's user preferences, demographics, and location, which makes them more relevant and effective.

Keep Your Tracking Ready

If you are going to invest in something, you should be able to keep track of your investment. Otherwise, there seems to be no point. If you are not able to see how well the ads you have placed are performing or where they seem to be lacking, then you should not spend money on paid advertisement. In traditional marketing, it is relatively harder to keep track of everything in the real world and in real time. But the beauty of the online world is that you can literally keep a track of everything in real time without having to bother with the hassle of moving or spending more money.

For example, if you own a car, then you cannot just go without checking it regularly, keeping it maintained, keeping an eye out for anything alarming, and so on. The same way, if you own an ad campaign that you have paid for, then it is your duty to make sure it runs smoothly. You can only do so by knowing everything about it.

Google Analytics is the best tool when it comes to keeping track of your online ads. It offers a single dashboard where you can create a custom campaign and keep an eye on the performance of that campaign with a wide range of statistics recorded.

Create a Landing Page

It is important for every website to have a lucrative homepage that is the center for all things and acts as the base for navigation. It is equally important to send the incoming traffic to your website to a landing page that is unique. At first, this may seem to be countering the existence of a homepage but there are a few reasons for using this strategy.

Firstly, landing pages can act as a link between the advertisements you place and your official website by creating a cohesive experience. This is done by customizing your message for incoming visitors and then the visitors can go to your website. It is sort of a meaningful welcome that makes the experience rich for the customer.

Secondly, these landing pages give you the ability to direct your customers more specifically to your website, where you want them to download a free E-book or sign up for something.

The third reason for having a landing page is quite simple: It makes tracking your visits very easy which is important for your digital records and marketing purposes.

Over time, when you use this strategy of using a landing page and combine the usage with some funnel tracking tools, you can have access to a lot of information about the kind of people that visit your site and what they are typically looking for. This can help you reach and sell to your visitors exactly what they want. One thing you have to remember is to block your custom landing page from search engines so that it does not show up in search results in any way. Having it linked to search engines will start giving you false information about how your page is performing.

Review Results Regularly

Reviewing results is a healthy activity in almost any area of business. But how often that you review data is more important because it varies from field to field. For digital marketing and advertisements, it is not a good idea to look at your results every day because this habit can keep building up pressure on you. Moreover, it may lead to you making certain changes too hastily. When running an ad campaign, it takes a certain time to hit the mark and you have to look at the average of results, instead of day-to-day results. You need to give time to your campaign to get noticed and start attracting traffic. You have to give time to your analytics to be able to gather certain trends and information which can only be done after keeping a track of the campaign but not changing anything in it. As you start using this, you will see there will be a certain amount of time taken to get a turnover. This will help you determine a set time period for reviewing your statistics.

Now that you have an idea of what paid advertising entails and along with the things you need to know before you start buying ads, I think we can take a deeper look into what paid advertising really does. In digital marketing, paid advertising involves paying the owner of an ad space online for the right to use that space. The negotiation of price for that ad space is commonly done by a bidding system where marketers and space owners bid for that space. The main categories of paid advertising include pay per click (PPC) or cost per click (CPC), pay per impression (PPI), and display advertisements.

We will look at display advertising more in the next chapter, where we will also discuss social media marketing. For now, it is vital that you know how PPC advertising works, or rather how Google Ads work.

Google Ads

Google Ads, previously known as AdWords is Google's own advertising service in the category of PPC advertising and is most widely used by all types of firms. This service allows users and owners of businesses to put their search results for their website on a Search Engine Results Page (SERP) by paying for them. Basically, the organic way of a website is to work its way up in the rankings over time but by using this paid service you can skip that part and show up near the top.

Type of Google Ads:
- Google Search Ads (google.com)

Google Search Ads have been the bread and butter of Google's revenue engine for quite some time. We may be seeing a shift into video and display ads taking this over in the near future.

Formerly known as Google AdWords, the platform allows for users to bid for the top placements in certain keyword search pages. It works as an auction, so the level of competition for certain keywords can vary greatly.

Take for example keywords having to do with finding a Mesothelioma lawyer, or asbestos cancer lawyer. (both are the same) Some keywords can cost upwards of $800 or more, per click! Compare that to a local shop that sells specialized items-- they could be paying on average around one dollar per click.

Winning in the auction is not only about bidding high, several other criteria must be met to consistently have the top spot on a keyword search. A certain 'quality score' Google assesses must be high. If it deems your score to be poor, you could wind up having to pay more for a top position, or not qualify altogether. You can raise your quality score by first making sure that your targeted keywords, ad copy, and landing page content are on topic. Anything that can be labeled as misleading will quickly be disap-proved by Google Ads' automated gatekeepers.

Secondly, your website should deliver a good user experience. This means that your text relevance, loading time, and mobile-friendliness all come into play. If any of these are off of their A-game, then you can expect a potentially lower score thus causing higher costs on your average CPC.

I like to recommend a Google Ads search campaign to those who want leads fast, and don't want to wait around to enjoy the benefits of organic SEO efforts.

The added value that this kind of marketing has over SEO is that if you are a Google user-- the paid section shows up above any organic ads. Throughout this book we cover more on configuring these efforts, and making the most out of advertising.

-Google Display Ads
(Google Ads on other sites via AdSense)

Once you have enough data from using Google search, you can launch your own banner campaign, which can be seen virtually anywhere a Google advertiser allows it. Perfect examples are major news sites, online magazine sites, and even Yelp are big participants in this.

To engage in this I recommend having a talented graphic designer available. There are some dimension guidelines to follow, and you'll need to get the same message across effectively through differing screen sizes.

Youtube Ads - Video Ads

Similar to Google Display ads, the video platform for Google allows you to be placed in many places throughout the web, and also allows you to target audiences in one of the busiest sites in the world-- YouTube. It's quite easy to guess what you need to start-- a YouTube video, of course! I'm sure you've seen now on your smart TV or smartphone a video automatically playing anytime something streams from YouTube-- these advertisers are actively using this platform. Of course, depending on your profile, i.e. what demographics and interest Google matches you up with-- you'll see different content from an array of advertisers. Say for example, if you watch music videos, you will likely get advertisements from other artists of a similar genre and their videos showing on YouTube, or even on a sponsored suggestion.

But say if you're a dentist-- This platform allows you to target people who have recently used Google to look for dentists. It matches you right up with them, and it also gives you the ability to put a custom call to action inside of the video and also direct them to your website.

In addition to this, the perk of this platform also is that it allows you to set many ways to bid and be billed--- for example-- do you want to pay a certain amount every time someone clicks, or someone hits a number of seconds on your video? Or would you like them to complete the video? In this case, you can be billed that way. There are many ways to stretch your budget on this platform. And best yet, by the numbers, video advertisements are known to convert at a much higher rate than anything that is text-based. More on this later.

- Google Play Store - App Ads

This form of advertising is becoming increasingly popular, and it becomes viewable in people's free apps that they download on their Apple or Google device.

So far what's been most popular, is to advertise applications on either the app store or within apps. This, in essence, pre-qualifies people who have the right kind of device.

Another ideal way to use this is if you do video advertising. This gets a fair amount of plays within people's unpaid apps.

I'd have to say, if you are a local business who doesn't have excellent branding videos, or other apps to download-- this can be a very wasteful part of the platform. As it turns out, false clicks are very prevalent in Google Play Apps. This is because they pop up so frequently, and with such speed-- that sometimes a user ends up clicking it on accident.

You should also watch out-- in many display campaigns, Google has been known to automatically include all app users on their targeting list. This has caused a large amount of people to run up a budget unnecessarily, because of the false clicks I've mentioned.

My main tip to you as an advertiser, is to exclude this unless you are an app marketer, or someone looking for mass video impressions. For an inexperienced advertiser, this process could be a bit technical, so call a professional for help if needed.

- Google Shopping
This is one of the more segmented niches of advertisers, because you have to be selling a physical good to qualify. As of right now, services do not qualify for this form of advertising.

This is Google's way (so far) of giving eBay and Amazon a run for their money. Any time a search is made for a closely-matched products on Google Shopping, the item is displayed right in the search results, seemingly available for instant purchase. For those with their cards saved with Google, this makes for an instant checkout, much like Amazon. For several like-products, like say, face cream-- the advertisers wil be displayed side to side, displaying each price and average number of review ratings.

In order to set this up, you must go to merchants.google.com and take all of the necessary steps to sync your website data with both your merchant account and Google Ads account. If you are in need of assistance from this, get some help, a good digital marketing firm like mine should be able to help.

- Gmail Ads

Gmail ads are an extension of a display campaign, but you have the ability to score "impressions" by many.

- Remarketing Ads

Remarketing is a prime way to stay fresh on a customer's mind. In my experience, it's also among the most cost-effective per interaction. This kind of targeting basically utilizes the 'cookies' that a website collects from users. Using these cookies-- such as IP address, frequent hot spots on the site, geographic location, and other key info, you can set a hyper-focused group to target on your ad campaign.

The best part, I believe, is that a remarketing campaign has the ability to follow your potential clients around to other sites that they like. It's just a matter of time until they land on a website that participates in Google's ad network-- and you'll be shown right there along with whatever clever copy or alluring banner you've conjured up with your creative.

Paid search is a term used to define the advertisements within a search engine - the ads you normally see at the top or side of the search results shown to you. Of course, Google is not the only one who provides this service but it is the most used so far. The basic principle that Google Ads operates on is the concept of keywords. So, the business owners or users pick a few keywords that a searcher may use on Google for something related to the business. Next, the advert is created which is linked to those keywords. Every time those keywords are typed in and searched for, the advert is shown along with other results. It is highly unlikely that you are going to be the only one with an advert based on certain keywords. Rival companies are allowed to bid for the same search term. This means that a SERP often has multiple adverts from different organizations. The more you pay per click, the more your advert appears in the search results.

The placement of adverts through Google Ads is not only based on this. It also uses something known as the quality score. Here, Google takes a look at your advert and gauges the quality based on relevance and usefulness to the searcher and the search terms linked to it. Another thing that is taken into account is the click-through rate along with the relevance of your landing page. For example, if your advert is for buying a specific product from your product range and it takes the searcher to the website's homepage, instead of the page for that product, then it is not relevant and useful to the potential customer. This produces a lower quality score.

Importance of Paid Advertising

For a marketing campaign to be efficient, it has to be able to capitalize on all channels that are available for advertising. Even though the cost for paid advertising is higher than having your own or earned advertising campaign, it does provide you with an effective way to promote your business' name to a much wider audience. Just think about it, how many places have you seen paid ads? They are usually displayed to online users on almost any part of the webpage. The benefit you have here apart from visibility is that over time, if you are able to pay more, then you can have your ads placed on more popular websites where traffic itself is generally higher. Furthermore, given the existence of different categories, you can further customize your ad campaign to better suit your client's needs.

The online advertising industry is a billion-dollar industry where the digital ad expenditure managed to reach over $137 billion in 2014. This accounts for one-quarter of all media spending. To gauge the importance and effectiveness of this, take a look at the following statistics.

1. 2013: The top three video advertisements managed to generate a total of more than 12 million shares.
2. 2013: Twitter delivered 400% more revenue per visit in 2013 than it did in 2011.
3. The click-through rate on average for Facebook managed to rise by 275% since 2012.

It is pretty clear that paid advertisement is an effective way of getting traffic to your website but since it is paid, you have to keep in mind that you get the right sort of traffic. In case your budget runs out, the traffic will stop coming in. Hence, you have only that window to establish yourself as a business so that you can earn advertisement after you stop investing in paid ads. It is rented advertisement, after all, so you have to be smart about it, because like many other things, the risk of losing your investment does exist here as well.

Online advertisement is also very attractive because it is measurable and highly sophisticated with regards to targeting. This means that it is actually possible to calculate both long-term and short-term values that how much revenue resulted from each and every incoming visit. It is also possible to target a very specific part of your demographics for more effective marketing.

Amazon PPC - Paid Marketing

SEO is not the only option Amazon give its users to rank on its SERPs. Amazon also created its own paid marketing system to make listings stand out from the rest. Amazon PPC is also known as 'Sponsored products". Paid ads on Amazon can be usually found above or below the organic results or in the right column. Just like in most of the regular PPC campaigns, a marketer would pay only for the ads users clicked on and generated views on the advertised product. Paid ads on Amazon also help improve organic rankings, if they're properly implemented on a regular basis.

Amazon marketplace gets millions of searches every month that go from short term to long term phrases (AKA keywords). Unlike traditional search engines, Amazon users are already there with a buying intention. Paid searches are strategically placed among the organic results in order to set aside of them. Each of these paid ads follow and enhanced auction-based approach. Sellers set a daily budget for each ad. The higher the bid, the higher the chances of the ad to stand out of others paid or non-paid. Still, listings require a proper level of optimization with the right use of keywords, relevant information and content in order to succeed. For more information, refer to the chapter "SEO for Amazon Store & Product Listings".

There are three main types of sponsored ads on Amazon:
1. **Sponsored product ads:** they allow a marketer to advertise products depending on a keyword. Thus, it is necessary to have an efficient keyword research to maximize its effect. These ads usually perform great when it comes to CTRs and conversions. These ads are usually displayed among the

organic searches.

2. **Product Display Ads:** these ads are shown in a similar product section on a product page. They are designed as a self-serving option that is paired with the ASIN (Amazon Standard Identification Number). Thus, this option gives marketers more options to focus on the behavioral segments. Product display ads have their own screen placement section and budgets. They differ in the CTRs and what influence them. With this type of ads, it's necessary to pay special attention on the type of product, the objectives and targeted audiences.

3. **Headline search ads:** also known as *banner ads*, they are limited to specific product categories. These are the ads that are usually seen on the top of search results with the brand logo. The main purpose of these ads is to lead buyers to click from a group of products. They also offer a high level of customization, as they allow to show many different products at the same time and customize the landing destinations. Marketers can also choose from their own brand pages, product pages, URLs and search result pages. Same applies to the images and text to display in the ads.

To use Amazon PPC, you require a seller account, be able to ship within the USA, meet the Buy Box eligibility criteria and comply with Amazon Brand Registry.

**Paid Marketing on Local Directories
(YELP, Google My Business)**

Local directories like Yelp and Google my Business have also grown in a way that they demanded paid options for their listings. Even though YELP is considered by many the most important review website, Google reviews is actually equally or even more important at the moment of influencing users to buy products or visit a business. Both websites generate such a level of awareness that almost necessarily lead to paid marketing.

Paid advertising on Yelp has certain particular characteristics. Yelp ads are displayed in several places including relevant search result pages and even competitor's Yelp pages. They also allow to display ads on different platforms such as desktop version, mobile Yelp site and mobile app. In recent updates, Ads on Yelp allow geotargeting.

There are two types of paid advertisements for businesses on Yelp: Business Page Upgrades and Yelp Ads. The first ones are premium features that make your Yelp profile look better. You can restrict your competitor's ads (which you're not allowed to do with the free listing), have an enhanced slideshow to organize the photos and a Call to action that allows to send coupons, order forms and other features to the visitors.

Yelp Ads, on the other hand, charge a specific amount of money for every click you receive on your listing. You can also get metrics on how your paid campaign performs. The main critic marketers have about Yelp paid options is that they lead very little traffic to the websites, as most of the users stay on Yelp website or app.

Google my Business also has a paid advertisement option, as it can be linked to Google Ads. This allows ads to appear with a business' physical location and be displayed on Google Maps search results. Aside of this, GMB has also some monthly paid features to help listings stand out. Some of these features are:

"Book" button on Google My Business profile: it allows users to check a business availability and book an appointment or consultation.

Promoted map pin: a special placement in Google maps when users are looking for businesses in your area.

Verified customer reviews: a very useful tool to make sure a user actually visited your location or bought your products.

Google guarantee: a trust badge to be displayed on your GMB profile that allows a customer to receive a refund from Google if he or she is not satisfied with your product or service.

Apple Ads - on App Store

Online stores featuring apps for mobile devices receive millions of visits every year. As per the first quarter of 2019 Apple's app store featured over 1.8 million apps. As we already covered in the chapter "SEO for Mobile Apps and ASO", such quantity and subsequent competitiveness between apps generated the need of ways to stand out from the rest and rank better. That's why along with the SEO for mobile apps the Apple ads appeared on the App Store.

These ads were introduced in 2016 as Search Ads. They were conceived to help developers target potential users using information like gender, location, keywords or if they downloaded the app before. One year later in 2017 Apple introduced "Search Ads Basic", a pay-per-install advertising product that was focused on smaller developers. Traditional Search Ads were also renamed as 'Advanced" to set a difference between both ways of doing paid advertising on the App Store.

After configuring your campaign Apple Ads are featured at the top of the App Store results when a user performs a query using a keyword that is related to the promoted app. The developer of the app pays for a different type of conversion depending on the Ad of choice. When using Advanced Search Ads, you pay every time a user taps on the app. On the other hand, Search Ads Basic demands a payment only when the app is installed in the user's device.

Just like any other pay per click campaign, Apple will suggest a maximum bid for certain keywords based on historical data from the App store about the type a developer intends to market. However, it doesn't build profiles or take individual's information to collect such data. The ads are featured exclusively at Apple's App store and nowhere else on the internet.

Search Ads also increase an account's organic rankings because Apple's algorithm counts the number of downloads and speed of install to rank an app. Apple takes an install from Search Ads as a high quality download. Thus, it raises an account general positioning. Even though there's no limitation on the type of ad and the size of the company bidding for it, Search Ads Basic has a limit of $5000 to bid. Advanced has no limit of money.

Apple's Search Ads are recommended for small developers who want to increase their app's exposure quickly and easily. Considering Search Ads have a Conversion Rate of more than 50% and a cost per acquisition below $1.50, Search Ads are among the most affordable and convenient Pay Per Click options on the internet.

Other paid marketing alternatives

Ever since Google pioneered the Pay Per Click model (and keeps on leading in that area), many forms of paid advertising flourished in time. We already discussed some of the most popular PPC options in previous chapters. Here, we will name some other not so known alternatives of paid advertising on the internet. Unlike your regular PPC campaigns, these paid marketing alternatives don't base on a website or listing performance in giant platforms like Google or Amazon. On the opposite, they base on each website behaviour and how that can attract bidders to pay ads on them.

Adroll

This is a digital marketing technology that specializes in retargeting; which means it bases its behaviour on the user's previous actions. Adroll uses different platforms like desktop and mobile sites as well as social media and allows you to create ads on them.

Media.net

Media.net builds products across multiple segments within ad tech. Thus, it intends to cover all of the user's needs without the intervention of multiple vendors. They claim to be "the original creators of the display-to-search (D2S) ad format" which monetizes display placements by identifying user search intent and showing relevant search keywords. These keywords lead to search ads that advertisers pay following a classic Cost Per Click model.

PropellerAds

A performance-driven advertising platform targeted for marketers and affiliates. This WordPress plugin allows site owners to monetize their entire mobile and web inventory: mobile apps, widgets, online games, software and more. It features several different tools for specific tasks like Push Notification, Native Banners, Smart Links among several others.

Adversal

Adversal is a CPM (cost per mille - which is the amount an advertiser pays a website for one thousand visitors converting on his or her ad). Its main characteristic is that it pays for each raw impression, not per visitor. Adversal' code allows its pop-under ads to not be easily blocked. Adversal is primarily used in North America.

Viglink

According to its website, Viglink promises to make every link on your website "intelligent and valuable". Its main target are bloggers, influencers and editorial sites. Viglink uses Natural Language Processing (NLP) technology to automatically link product mentions on articles and other content to the best-paying bidding marketers.

Skimlinks

This content monetisation platform also targets content from forums, bloggers, editorial websites but it also contemplates pp developers. Skimlinks specializes on in-text contextual advertising: it focuses on particular keywords within the content that is matched with related ads.

In the next chapter we will discuss more about Social Media Marketing, as another channel of Paid Ads.

Chapter 7

Social Media Marketing

5 key strategies to get you started sucessfully

1. Focus on one channel first.
   Get good at it.
   Then focus on the next

2. Use social media account management
   tool to automate your tasks

Hootsuite™

≋ buffer

socialoomph

3. Dedicate time to create content
   Repurpose Content into multiple blogs
   to ebooks and videos to podcasts

4. Run contests
   Conduct giveaway campaigns
   Offer exclusive discounts
   through product promotions.

Content   Blogs   Ebooks/Videos   Podcast

5 Opt for Facebook advertising, Instagram ads, etc

Facebook Ads

Ads

In order to gain an understanding of social media marketing, you need to be drawn in on everything we went over in the previous chapters. This includes building an online presence, online reputation management, and paid advertising as well since social media marketing includes all of this. The term social media refers to all the sites that are able to provide differing forms of social interactions among users, such as Twitter, where you can share short messages or updates with other users. Then there's Instagram, where users can upload pictures and edit them to form a public library, and Facebook, which is a full social networking site that has all of these features and more.

What Is Social Media Marketing?

Social media marketing makes use of specific major social media sites since they have the most number of registered users. Essentially, it is a form of internet marketing that makes use of these sites as a marketing tool by producing content that the users share on their own social networks. This helps marketers reach their goal of increasing brand awareness and exposure along with widening their customer base and driving more customers to their own websites. As we discussed before, one of the main components of search engine marketing was search engine optimization. Similarly, the key component of social media marketing is social media optimization.

Marketers draw up strategies tailored to each of the social media platforms, according to how they function. This is in order to draw new and unique visitors to their sites.

This can be done in two ways. Either by adding social media links to their content in the form of

RSS feeds or sharing buttons, or by promoting activity through social media by updating content in the form of tweets, blogs, or statuses. In short, social media marketing is a form of internet marketing that aims to achieve the exposure goals of a company.

Over time, social media marketing has become more common considering the fact that the popularity of social media sites has risen. As it grew, the Federal Trade Commission had to update its rules to allow space for social media marketing. Now, if a company decides to provide a blogger or any other social media user any sort of free products in order to promote it and get it shared on social media, then it must also know that the online comments that the activity gets are going to be legally treated as an endorsement. Hence, for the company and the person sharing the promotional content, it is imperative that they insure the incentives and clearly disclose that the posts contain no misleading information of any sort. Basically, the rules for normal marketing apply here so that there is no room for deceptive advertising.

It is also important to understand the relationship between search marketing and social media marketing, because both are the forms of online marketing and are also closely related. Search marketers care about what goes on the social media, so the search engines scour the social media for things to display in their search results. The thing is, social media is the source of new content or updated content through news stories, blogs, and other various types of posts. Hence, when search engines look through everything available on the Internet, social media becomes an important area to look through because they might be able to discover something new about someone.

Social media also acts as a link builder that helps support the efforts of search engine optimization. SEO uses links to direct customers and the social media posts have tags and links embedded in them. Numerous people perform searches on social media sites for content that they know exists on a given platform. Every social media site has an option to search its site for almost anything new. If people are using that search option, then they are also getting search results in response to their search. If search engines link up to these sites, then they can also be used for the same searches. The relevancy of search results on these sites is also affected by social connections, either within a social media network or on a mainstream search engine.

Benefits of Using Social Media Marketing

Social media marketing has a growing role in the world. Your business and clientele can take advantage of it by attracting a wide array of untapped customers. The large social media platforms give access to insurmountable possibilities if it is effectively utilized. Using social media marketing can vastly improve the amount of exposure that your company gets with a much lower cost. Think of spending as little as one hour a day every week to raise your business' traffic and sales at minimal cost.

Even though social networks are now a vital part of every marketing strategy and it is easy to see why social media marketing factors into success, a lot of professionals in the industry are still unsure of what strategies and tactics to use. According to a survey done by Social Media Examiner, it was found that around 96% of the marketers were using social media marketing in one way or the other, but 85% of these marketers did not know which tools were the best option for them to use. Over the next section, we will go over the clear advantages of using social media to clear up the confusion.

Over the course of this chapter, we will be going through techniques and strategies that will help create a strong social media presence. First, let us have the prime focus on going through why social media presence is so important for any brand. It is a general rule of thumb that when someone knows and understands the importance of something, then they are more likely to have a sharper focus on what they do with that thing, how creative they become with it, and how they treat it generally. Once you have the importance of this in your mind, it will be much easier to focus and tailor the techniques and strategies that we discuss further for your own brand.

1. **Rise in Brand Awareness:** It seems that without any argument, social media is one of the most cost-effective ways of digital marketing to increase your brand's visibility in the online world. Content that is produced to be posted on social media is connected to a social media strategy that is able to improve your brand recognition because it engages with a much larger number of consumers unlike in search marketing. It is very simple to get started by building a social media profile for your business and to begin interacting with other users. However, it is advisable that you start by making a profile on one social media site first and then the others in order to get the hang of how each site functions. The next step is to simply ask your employees, sponsors, business partners, and everyone to like and share your page or profile. This counts as interacting with

your content since it will be showing up in the newsfeed and it may lead to a new network of users. Investing only a few hours in this in the beginning will help build your profile to be notice-able.

2. **Rise in Inbound Traffic:** Have you ever seen a shepherd gather sheep and drive them toward where he wants them to go? Maybe not in real life but in a movie for sure. If you have, then you have probably seen the shepherd on a horse, a few dogs around the herd of sheep or cows, and a few of the cattle straying from the herd as the herd moves toward the enclosure. This is pretty much how your social media accounts will work. The main website is your main enclosure where you have set everything up for consumers to interact with.

    *   The social media accounts are the dogs that help you keep the herd moving toward where you want them to go. When you create a website or add a new page to your website, it is like taking an amazing picture of yourself. You want the whole world to see it but since it is yours, you do not want to beg for attention. This is where your social media accounts come in. You can use them to divert traffic into your ecosystem to this new website or page.

    *   Every social media account is different. A well-placed and well-thought-of post on one of these social media accounts can make a big difference. You can spice up curiosity in the consumers, or you can leave them hanging so they have to see more. You can also make an offer that they cannot refuse.

Rise in Search Engine Rankings: In the introduction to digital marketing, I talked about what search engine optimization is and how it is an important tool for digital marketers. Search engine optimization works by showing results for a website or brand that has constant or higher traffic than others. Search engine crawlers know which pages are being visited more or are consistently earning traffic and which pages are just floating out there on the internet space. If you come up with a good content or advertising strategy for your brand's SEO, it is sure to raise the importance of your brand so that it is able to earn top spots in the search engine rankings. However, that is not the only way to earn higher rankings. If you combine these strategies with the practice of using your social media accounts in such a way that consumers or users are always interacting with your posts in one way or the other or are being diverted to your website, then this will make you climb up in the search engine rankings much faster. The simple reason is that your social media accounts will be linked to your website and any post that you make on your social media accounts will contain keywords and links to your website so obviously that it will show up in search engine crawlers. All you need is a consistent social media presence on Facebook, Twitter, and Instagram and of course, your website as well.

Relationship Building: In the past, most of the world agreed that any sort of real relationship building could only be done in real time and in each other's physical presence. This was true to an extent since the technology was not as evolved as it has now. The issue of talking and communicating in real time is gone now and most of the world's population that you target is already on the Internet. The tools that you would use to make your communication stronger in each other's presence also exist on the Internet. For example, finding the location and nearby places, knowing what something or someone looks like, preferences, behaviors and even just waving at someone as you pass by them. With the rising use of technologies, you have a chance of using them in the right way and establishing real relationships with your consumers just the way you would have if they actually entered your showroom or warehouse. In fact, you can do much more.

Moreover, with the use of social media accounts like Twitter and Instagram, the interaction you have with your customer base is personalized as well. You can read their posts and tweets, look at their pictures, and get an insight into their daily lives. This will help you judge them and tweak your marketing strategies according to your analysis of them. For example, you can find out what they are doing on the weekend, what places they like to visit, and what their interests are. Things like these open up a vast number of opportunities to do. Things like offering promotions based on their interest, offering discounts at places they like, and so on. Another opportunity to expand your ecosystem and build a dominating presence arises here, as you can also build a real relationship with other brands. Not only this, but you can also connect with journalists, public speakers, experts in your industry and so on.

Users Become More Receptive to Your Message: The good thing about social media accounts is that they are still used for personal networking and not viewed as marketing platforms only. These accounts have a lot of privacy settings as well to keep advertisements out of the way. People who are using these accounts do not only see your posts as pure marketing efforts but also pay more attention to what message you are trying to get across.

Usually, advertisements that keep popping up or are placed to fill spaces have their messages discarded by the consumer unless the consumer is specifically looking for them. However, when certified forums or the friends share links to your brand or talk about it, then they will be more likely to hear what you have to say.

Getting Started

You now have a hang of social media management and how it works. You know the importance, you know the terms, you know the differences and advantages, and you know how to start building a social media presence for your brand. The question that remains is how to dominate social media and what kinds of tips and tricks you can use to make your strategies better. The following strategies will get you started and give you an idea of what you should do.

1. Dominate one channel first, get good at it, and then expand your presence to other channels. Managing more than one channel in the beginning can become very tiring. You can lose out on a good consumer base since you will not be able to focus everywhere at once or you will need a social media manager which can be costly in the beginning.

2. The second step is to get your tasks automated. You can use social media account management tools such as Buffer, Hootsuite, and SocialOomph to expand your presence. You can use a content calendar to decide which posts to upload on what day and at what time.

3.   Take one piece of content and repurpose it into blogs. Take multiple blogs and convert them into ebooks and videos, transcribe them into audio podcasts, or tweet important bullet points.

4.   Dedicate a couple of days a month to creating multiple videos or multiple blogs. After this, you can apply content repurposing on them as well.

5.   Run contests, conduct giveaway campaigns, and offer exclusive discounts through product promotions.

6.   Opt for Facebook advertising, Instagram ads, etc.

Facebook & IG Ads
(Lead Ad, FB messenger)

One of the more popular ads in 2019 has been with Facebook messenger. It allows people to view an ad and immediately be put in touch with an agent on the other side, all through facebook. We have utilized this with several clients, and this is particularly useful among lawyers, for example.

Facebook and Instagram Ads

Ads on Facebook and Instagram have become increasingly popular in recent years. Even though they apply to all sorts of industries, eCommerce stores are among the main beneficiaries of paid ads in such platforms.

Facebook Ads

Paid ads on Facebook present different options. A marketer can promote a Facebook Page, specific posts on such a Page or a website. Even though Facebook Ads tend to focus on advertising within the platform, they are a very fruitful way to send traffic to an external website. Facebook ads targeting includes user's demographic, location and profile information. When a marketer creates an ad, a budget is set to bid for each click it receives or per thousand impressions. Facebook Ads are usually visible on Facebook' sidebar.

Ads on Facebook characterize for being better to generate a demand than for fulfilling it. Unlike search engines or buying platforms where users have a specific intention, Facebook primary intention is to connect people; not to answer a query or purchase products per-se. Marketing on Facebook (and thus, paid ads) are heavily related to the interest content that is shared in their specific pages. A successful marketing on Facebook is subtle. And when it comes to paid ads it's more recommendable to lead to conversions that lead to sales instead of sales themselves.

Instagram Ads

This is probably the most visual of all massively popular social media platforms, as it's purely based on photos, short videos, 'stories' and little to none written content. Instagram is the platform of choice of the millennial generation and demographics in the early forties and below. As Facebook owns Instagram, you can use Facebook data to target audiences on Instagram. Businesses can interact with users through ads mostly in the home page and the comment section of the photos.

Instagram presents a total of six ad formats to choose from. Four of them are Instagram feed ads and two, Instagram stories ads:

Feed Ads:

- **Photo Ads:** they feature one image and can be featured in a group of six ads with one different image each.
- **Video Ads:** they can be added in video format or GIF
- **Slideshow Ads:** video ads in a loop featuring up to 10 images. It can include music.
- **Carousel Ads:** two or more images or videos.

Stories ads

- **Single image:** allowing up to six ads with one different image each.
- **Single video:** 15 seconds long video or GIF

Pinterest Ads

Pinterest is hands down one of the most curious platforms in social media, heavily based on discovery and navigation. Most of its images are not branded, which makes easier for Pinterest users to open up to new products and ideas. Paid ads on Pinterest have certain particularities that are linked to such exploration and discovery trends. It is also worth mentioning that such ads are available only in the USA, Canada, the United Kingdom, Australia, Ireland, France and New Zealand.

There are up to seven different types of Pinterest Ads available:

Promoted Pins

They are usually placed in the home feed and search results along with regular Pins. HOwever, they are boosted and targeted in such a way that they have a wider reach. They also feature a "Promoted" label. Aside of this particularity, they look and behave like any other regular Pin. They can be Pinned on user's boards, shares and get comments.

One-tap Pins

Starting 2019 all Pinterest ad feature this one-tap system; meaning that when someone taps or clicks an ad, they're directed straight to a landing page.

Promoted Carousels

Promoted Carousels consist in a group of two to five images that Pinterest users can swipe through. Each image can feature a different description, title and landing page; which makes it ideal to promote multiple products that somehow relate. The carousels ads have the same behaviour as a regular pin, except that they feature dots indicating the swipe option.

Promoted Video Pins

Very similar to the Promoted Pins except that they feature video instead of static photos. They also show in the home feed, search results, and the "more like this" section. Video pins autoplay when they're 50 percent in view. Pinterest allows two sizes: Max width and standard videos.

Promoted App Pins

They allow users to download a mobile app directly from Pinterest. They also look and act like the Promoted Pins except that they link to an App Store or Google Play app store URL. They also feature an install button. Promoted App Pins are only available for mobile users.

Buyable Pins

These Pins allow users to find and buy products directly from a Pin that is related to them. Available for both desktop and mobile users, they are placed in the same sections as the Promoted Pins.

Story Pins

Story Pins can show up to 20 pages of images, links and text. They are shown in users' home feeds featuring a cover image and a title; with a "Story" underneath. These Pins can be saved to user's boards like any other Pin.

LinkedIn Advertising

LinkedIn works a little bit different than say, Facebook, because the user base is all under a professional hat. So in a way, this is a good way to hyper-target people one a B2B basis, or to provide professional services. One of the things I recommend doing on LinkedIn for brand awareness is sponsoring notifications for people to follow your business.

But don't let those efforts go to waste-- if you pay for a following-- keep them informed. This doesn't cost you any money. Give them insights about your company, like articles that give an added value. If you don't do this, you risk people unfollowing you.

LinkedIn is the social media that capitalizes a very specific niche: business professionals. One platform that initially was intentioned to find a new job or employees eventually turned into a highly useful tool for inbound marketing. This phenomenon came hand-in-hand with the creation of LinkedIn Ads. As it networks professionals and businesses alike, LinkedIn can monetize ads by making a business reach potential clients and decision makers with specific content that is implemented in paid ads. What's mostly offered most of the times is services, as of course that's what a professional usually has to offer but it's also very common to promote software and other goods.

To start using LinkedIn Ads, it's necessary to first set a campaign up. LinkedIn advertising is in a separated platform than a regular profile. Such platform is called LinedIn Marketing Solutions. Once there, you can create the ads by simply clicking on the corresponding button. After you create your Campaign Manager account, you can create your campaigns, which can be organized through Campaign groups. You can set your objectives, which means what you intend users to do with the ads: visit a website, engage users to participate in polls or following a LinkedIn page, increase exposure on a video or generate a lead using an online form.

Once the objectives of the campaign are set, the next step is to establish the parameters of the target audience. LinkedIn supports a wide range of options to customize the ads to very specific audiences; starting with up to 20 different languages available. Geolocation is also available, from wider options like nationwide to more specific like counties, cities and even locations nearby the area you;re targeting. Demographics, level of education, industry and areas of interest are among the many criteria your campaign on LinkedIn can follow.

Linkedin Ads support several different formats:

- **Text ads:** text only ads that feature in the right column or the top of the LinkedIn site.
- **Single image ads:** one image that appears on the newsfeed along with organic content.
- **Carousel ads:** two or more images also on the newsfeed.
- **Video ads:** one video on the LinkedIn newsfeed.
- **Follower ads:** available just for desktop, these ads are useful to promote a LinkedIn Page using a profile data to customize the ad.
- **Spotlight ads:** used for special offers, they also use LinkedIn profile data and are desktop only.
- **Job ads:** they promote open positions using LinkedIn profile data. They're only available on LinkedIn desktop too.
- **Message ads:** delivered to profiles that match a target audience to their LinkedIn inbox.

Other Social Media Ads
Twitter Ads

Due to its nature (a platform that allows quick, short messages) Twitter Ads can be used for three main purposes: to attract new followers, drive traffic and conversions to a specific website or generate and capture leads. There are also certain specific types of ads on Twitter. Promoted tweets are tweets that a marketer pays to display and thus engage new followers. Promoted Accounts, as it name indicates, advertises a Twitter account targeting on users who don;t follow it yet. Promoted Trends are particularly useful to enhance hashtags and thus generate trending topics. Twitter Ads can be automated using Twitter

Promote Mode, which for a flat cost of u$s99 will auto-matically promotes the first ten daily tweets on your account to selected audiences.

Youtube Ads

Since it was purchased by Google, Youtube depends on Google Ads in order to create its paid advertisements. Youtube ads are particularly useful to generate leads, attract traffic to a website, generate product and brand awareness and extend their reach. Video ads formats are not necessarily varied but very specific. TrueView Ads automatically play before, during or after a video and give the option to skip after five seconds. They generally last up to 30 seconds and can also feature in other places of Google's display network like apps or games. Non-Skippable You-Tube ads, of course, cannot be skipped and last up to 20 seconds. They are featured at the beginning or in the middle of videos that last more than ten minutes. Bumper Ads can't be skipped either but last up to six seconds, appearing at the end of Youtube videos.

Snapchat Ads

Along with Instagram, Snapchat is the social media of choice for the millennial generation. Also like Instagram, it's practically based on mobile so Snap-chat ads are aimed to generate app downloads or engage users within the platform to discover and follow brand or individual's profiles. Snap Ads come with the format of mobile interactive videos that are usually implemented to promote apps or mobile games. Sponsored lenses give brands the opportunity to create their own filters for users to use while promoting the company. Snapchat Discover places a company's story at the top of user app feeds. These three Snapchat ads options are considerably expensive, costing the Snap Ads between $1,000 to $3,000 per month; $450,000 to $700,000 per day the Sponsored lenses and $50,000 per day for Snapchat Discover. So it's deductible that only big names can afford these advertisements.

Tumblr Ads

Heavily based on blogs and written content, Tumblr generates a very particular bond between users and brands. Sponsored Posts are ads featured in users' dashboards that look and feel like organic content. Sponsored Video Posts follow the Sponsored Posts format but implementing audiovisual content. Sponsored Day ads allow a brand to pin their logo and tagline to the top of all Tumblr users' dashboards for 24 hours.

Reddit Ads

This platform specializes in AMAs (ask me anything) and viral content. It works as an open forum to discuss all sorts of topics. Although it may not seem like a popular social media, it is actually used by 6% of all adults on the internet. Unlike most of the social media, Reddit targets audiences throughout subreddits: internal niche communities related to specific groups of people and topics. Reddit ads formats are: Promoted post, subdivided in link ads and text ads; and Display ads, which is a traditional online display ads in the form of a banner or rich media.

Chapter 8

Customer Relationship Managers (CRMs)

Customer Service

Sales

CRM

Marketing

Technical Support

Now that we've gone through most of today's leading methods of capturing leads via Digital Marketing, let's talk about how to manage, track, and retain them once they enter your sphere. If we are to make full use of the best of today's technology to give us a competitive edge, then the use of a Customer Relationship Manager should be a serious consideration.

There is a reason the chapter for CRM comes in chapter 8, however. If you have only enough clients to count on your fingers, your business is not quite scaled to the point that it needs a CRM. However, let's say you're taking a high volume of leads and calls in a given day, and there are issues with taking records or following up-- this is where it becomes very useful.
The most popular CRMs you may have heard of are Sales Force, Hubspot, Insightly, Agile, and there are plenty more in this competitive field.

So what is a CRM?

It is a cloud based software/platform in which data from your customer interactions are recorded. A good CRM makes for various methods of intake and has a good amount of integrations with things such as email, phone calls, contact forms, third party inquiries, and other lead funnels. It is a great way to set tangible goals as a team, like with sales, signups, phone calls, POS data, etc. This is because CRMs can clearly define special goals and track them in real time-- all on the cloud.

How to use a CRM

Practical use of most of today's CRM's is quite easy to use and to get a hold of. However, some higher functions such as automations and integrations might require training or help from an experienced web programmer.

In my personal experience, it seems most constructive for me to *dabble* with as many functions that I can while getting familiar with a new software. This allows me to gain some quick reflexes and know where everything is while I work on it.

Most users can take advantage of tracking customers by making use of customized fields that log key information on them. Upon first interaction with a customer, you can log as much information as you care to solicit from them and input it into your contacts categories. When you save it, it creates a file on this person. From here on you will be able to track and profile their journey they take with you as a customer.

Here is where I find that key data becomes tedious and overlooked. When you create that file, you cannot have you or your staff continue interacting with this person at later times without properly lagging it in your CRM. Not doing so creates lost opportunity of how the CRM is able to help you. By not updating the correct customer file, you lose valuable infor- mation that can be followed up on, or referenced by colleagues at a later time.

What's wonderful about CRM systems is that it allows you to mark, classify, and segment your cus- tomer base in any way you please. For example, you can filter a small group of your most loyal clients for a rewards program by simply setting a few rules on that identifies them on your CRM. You can mark custom- ers according to what kind of service, product, or sub- scription they currently receive. As a scaling company in higher phases of growth, this becomes important, because clients can be followed up on by anyone on your team who is available-- not just a dedicated person.

Find a CRM Tailored Towards Your Industry

If you are in the medical, real estate, financial, or manufacturing industries, you may want to seek out specialized CRM's that are made to specifically address the needs in your field. If you are opting to use one of the major platforms, do your due diligence and find out if they support the intake of the type of data you need to collect, or would like to collect. For example, some CRM's have the ability to integrate and plugin with a hospital's healthcare system, or with an automated manufacturing production report. These are just specific examples. But the point here is that not all of these CRM companies offer every integration. Also, in some cases, higher features are a significant markup, so find out which one is right for your business.

Best Practices

It's important to log as much of your client interactions as possible. This will give you an overall barometer if your clients are hot or cold as a group. By using CRM data, you can identify trends in slow business times, underperforming agents, clients favorite services or products, and much more.

This gives much added value to any business owner or manager. Using this data enables you to gather data that is actionable, and make proper adjustments to fine-tune business performance.

For example, you can create sales leader boards, assess leads by scores or deal amounts, or compare performances based on any dates you set. Best yet, many CRMs today give you the ability to easily turn these data points into presentable reports that can be downloaded or printed.

Sales

A CRM System is an added value to any sales

team. In fact, many sales teams are now turning to CRMs in droves as their primary tool for selling. When a lead or prospect comes in, many sales professionals are on their computer, adding every bit of information into the CRM. Most platforms out there will allow for a sales or intake person to set appointments with prospects, make follow up alerts, and track their progress and deal amounts.

This becomes especially useful when a company is generating a high amount of phone calls or leads. Depending on the need a client expresses, they can be passed on to a specialist, and that specialist can have a good amount of customer information available already on the CRM.

This has become the best way to monitor activity and also document any negotiations that may be happening with a client. Each company's sales process may differ, so CRM systems allow for you to create certain stages that your sales team or customers might go to. Take for example (in negotiations, creating audits, or application in process.

Emails

This ties in nicely to the theme of sales. If you happen to have a sales force that relies on sending emails to prospects and clients, then

In earlier CRM days, you were able to log that you sent an email, and perhaps paste in the message, or a summary of what it contained. Today, it is one of the easier integrations to make on most platforms is that with your inbox. To integrate your email with a CRM, suggest using Outlook, G-mail, or G-Suite as your primary client, as they integrate more seamlessly with most platforms. If you happen to be using a more customized mail server, you may need to get your IT person involved in integrating the accounts.

Once there, you have another advantage. All emails will be logged in the CRM, thus creating a more complete timeline in your client communications process. You will also be able to track any email you send-- as the CRM can provide you with alerts when an email recipient reads your message, and how many times they have opened it.

Indeed, CRMs have given sales teams in the business world a considerable amount of tools that have never been available before.

As a Sales Funnel

A CRM system can be molded as you please. You can use it to integrate with your major existing sales funnel, or it can become your primary sales funnel.

In most cases, you are able to automatically upload data that came in through forms on your website or even other places. Most of the Major CRM solutions have this feature available. To fully integrate it in a seamless way make require the help of a web developer.

You can also program some lead capture forms within the CRM system. In some cases, it can be inserted into your website, or it can generate a dedicated URL for capturing leads.

For example, our web agency uses HubSpot. Although we have our website contact forms integrated with our HubSpot, I have also created an appointment calendar for myself and all of my staff. By giving this link out to prospects, they voluntarily provide their main contact information into a form in exchange for some 1-on-1 meeting time with me.

Landing Pages

Some CRMs like Agile and HubSpot also allow you to design web pages right on the platform. This is becoming a more common feature on many of the major CRM solutions today. You will be able to create custom landing pages that contain lead capture forms that are directly tied in to your contacts database.

Although many are limited to a few templates, each give you the flexibility to tinker with the elements and add your touch in the form of text, photos, and videos.

If you are thinking about implementing this, I suggest that you A/B test it alongside your other lead generation forms. Let the market decide which is more appealing and more accessible.

Mobile Apps

Professionals can rejoice in the fact that many CRMs have developed mobile apps, enabling all client affairs and pending cases to follow you outside of the office. This may sound exciting or petrifying, depending on your level of dedication. Of course, each of these platforms will give a good level of control as to what you get alerted about.

Depending on your settings, you can receive push notifications that you have received a new lead, a new email, an urgently marked matter, a task, or an appointment. You can turn these on and off as you please. This can be particularly useful for a salesperson, who will be alerted the instant a new lead comes in.

Among the competitive world of CRM systems, some have better phone apps than others. HubSpot, for example, contains scanner that can create a contact by simply pointing the phone's camera to a business card. You are also able to send and receive messages and emails through most of these apps. One thing that I found consistent among different apps is the ability to update data and statuses of customers in the database

CRM systems tie in directly to what the following chapter will cover: email marketing. This is because a CRM platform can be among the most useful tools in gathering and segmenting a very strong email list. All of your staff's diligence in taking copious notes will pay dividends in the way a nice email list pans out

If you as a business administrator that is fully committed to your CRM, you will find a good number of customers mountining in your database. You can then easily export all of your contacts and place them into your Constant Contact or MailChimp recipients list. Some CRM companies are even developing the mail client to be included as a part of their system. Some providers now have options to design your own newsletter template and pull a list of any size into the recipients' list.

How to Decide on a CRM

As previously stated, deciding on the right CRM for your company depends on your industry and which CRM on the market provides the best solution for your needs. Many CRM providers offer free trial runs of their software, so I encourage interested parties to take the time to try them out. My company has used several CRM systems in recent years, and each of them have their pros and cons.

I said at the beginning of the chapter that CRMs are not for all businesses. You have to have grown to a considerable size as a small business to begin making good use of a CRM system. If you're not quite sure if you've gotten there, make use of a free trial that most of these major providers offer. Get a feel for yourself as to whether it will help your business. This shouldn't take you long, because as you experience each of the simplest of features, you will know whether using the platform will save you time and/or money.

Also, make sure you have a large list of your clients exported into a nice readable file, so that we can get into the following chapter about the dynamics of email marketing.

Chapter 9

Email Marketing

5 Steps to Doing it Right

1. Get Permission

Give users a reason to submit their email address

2. Use an email marketing platform

MailChimp

AWeber
EMAIL MARKETING DELIVERED

Constant Contact

Get white listed

3. Segment Emails

segmentation means splitting up your client list on the basis of relevant details in to smaller groups that you can target

4. Pay attention to email analytics

Analyze
· Open rates
· Click through rates
· Unsubscribe rates

5. Follow up emails

Create follow up emails
Set an autoresponder

How many of you remember the times when mail was still used as the most popular and common forum for an exchange of messages? Maybe some of us remember the newsletters that we had from our school or maybe some of us remember writing to our grandparents. We are far away from it now and the next generation will most probably not remember hearing the words "You've got mail", but they will most definitely see it on the screens of their laptops and phones.

Mail is one of the most important pieces formed in the history of the Internet that shifted everything that could be done through normal mail by post. It added a whole lot of new features to it while the road was still being discovered and the world was stumbling across the new web. The times have changed drastically and you probably no longer get things in your mail like CD's and letters but there was a time when mailing was the most elaborate platform for a lot of things. I remember that car dealerships used to mail my father brochures for new models and promotions while my mother used to similarly receive a lot of letters from her many social activities and groups.

In today's world, we have managed to replace all of that with much simpler and yet more complex platforms like Tweets, status updates and likes. The activity on these has increased so much so to the point that now it seems that our affinity for email is not any less.

That is quite a surprising thought but it is also true. For an average person like me, I remember when I was sending and receiving messages on Facebook messenger, Twitter, Instagram direct messages and even Snapchat but it started getting too much and so whenever I wanted to send something that was not causal or work related I chose to stick to email.

The fact is that, since there is so much noise now on social media, it is easy to argue that the email inbox you have, it is more of a personal space for people, a place of solitude amongst the online world.

This is the reason why focusing on email marketing and building a successful email marketing campaign is more important than ever since that is the only place where you are really away from all of the noise of the online world. The problem is, a lot of people do not realize this important and do not know how to do it right.

Do not think that the Internet has made things easy for you-- in fact just like traditional marketing where mail by post was used to market promotions and goods after careful research, you will have to do the same for email marketing as well. Before we look at how to carefully build an email marketing campaign from the grassroots level, let's make sure we have a complete understanding of what email marketing really entails.

What exactly is email marketing?

Email marketing is something that has become an essential tool for business marketing ever since the introduction of the online world. It can be categorized as a form of direct marketing and is essentially there to help you connect with your audience to promote your brand and raise sales. So basically what you are trying to do is use electronic mail to communicate commercial or fundraising messages to an audience that you have selected. This means that potentially, every email that a business sends to a current customer or a person can be considered email marketing but more specifically, the term is used to refer to either of the following three things:

1. Sending emails with the aim to better the relationship of a merchant with its current or previous customers so that you potentially have future business with them.

2. Sending emails with the target of getting new customers for your business or for convincing existing customers to purchase something immediately.

3. Sending emails that have been sent by other companies and adding advertisements to them.

So as you can see, there are a lot of things that can be accomplished with email marketing if done right. You can sell products, share news, tell a story, acquire new customers and so on but the main purpose of email marketing is the same as other marketing techniques, to increase brand loyalty, to get customers to make purchases and to enhance the relationship with existing customers.

The pros and cons of email marketing

Like all other facets of digital marketing, email marketing too has its own unique set of benefits and drawbacks and it is a good idea to get to know the most important ones before learning how to successfully run an email marketing campaign. As amazing as the return on investment for email marketing may be, which is what most digital marketers talk about when discussing the advantage of email marketing; it does not mean that it is enough to always outweigh the drawbacks. You have to figure out if email marketing is going to be specifically advantageous to your kind of campaign or your kind of business which is why in the next section we will go over the process of launching an email marketing campaign. Granted that the return on investment is the highest for email marketing, there are other added benefits as well as some drawbacks:

To start off with, an important pro of email marketing is that it is relatively measurable. When looking at any kind of marketing effort, there needs to be some sort of measurability to gauge the reach and the success of the efforts. Without any measurability, you would not know how many people clicked on your advertisement, website or newsletter. For emails, the likelihood of people actually opening your email depends on a number of factors such as the length of the subject line, the authority of the sender, the magnet words and the number of campaigns. For example, sending too many email campaigns in a month may mean that the email open rates decline.

According to research, the apt number of emails differs for B2B and B2C businesses but generally the email channel has found to have the ability for highest measurement of return on investment. Search and online advertisements come next in line with the highest ability to track and measure.

Another advantage of email marketing is the ability to personalize the marketing email. In fact, the sound of sending as many personalized emails as you want is very appealing to some marketers. Adding personalized touches is also one of the ways to increase the revenue you can generate because personalized emails mostly increase the click rates of consumer products and services. It also goes without saying that in order to be able to send authentic personalized emails, you have to be able to collect as much data as possible about your customers.

It has been said that personalized emails have a higher chance of being opened. For example, instead of just saying Hello in an email, adding a "Hello" with the name of the person you are sending it to will catch the person's attention.

Finally, the art of segmentation can also be addressed through email marketing and you will see that for a successful email marketing campaign, you will also have to address the issue of segmentation. For every business, there are going to be customers who spent more than average but have not bought anything in a long time. To be able to get through to these, you will need to segment these customers so that you can approach specific groups in a better way but for that you will also need more information about them. Segmenting emails makes your emails more relevant, but it also lowers the unsubscribe rates and through emails you can segment on the basis of demographics and interests, and so on. This makes it possible to approach the customers who haven't bought anything in a while separately.

However, all of these benefits come at a cost, one of which is having deliverability issues. This means that your traffic has grown, so much so that you now need to make sure that your emails are reaching the inbox directly. The deliverability rate is important if you are sending a large number of emails every month and sometimes it is wise to buy a dedicated IP address which lets you keep your authority safe. Sending too many emails can get you on the

SPAM blacklist which means that you have a problem.

Time constraint is another drawback that you will have to face because you simply cannot build an emailing list overnight. It will take time and that is sometimes the biggest issue with email marketing because marketers are unable to invest enough time in building that list. One of the best ways to deal with this problem is by generating leads through different methods that lead to your site but once there, the customers will have to provide an email address to see the results. Blogging is a good way to generate leads and you will be able to get a lot of new subscribers by combining blogging with other methods like conferences, webinars or Facebook advertisements. There are numerous other ways to get leads as well, but the trick is to not allow the customers to see the results until they provide an email address.

One of the other drawbacks I noticed in email marketing was linked to the increased use of mobile phones in today's age. Most emails are now opened on a mobile device which means that for the marketer, worrying about the design issue for your emails and attachments is necessary because people are most likely to open it on their phones and they are also likely to lose interest if the media or newsletter is not responsive on their phones. You have to be very careful about everything in the email you are sending, even the subject line. Checking how your email is going to appear on a phone is necessary because it is very plausible that the subject line is not going to be wholly visible when viewed on a phone and the amount of it going to be visible is going to vary from phone to phone as well.

Step 1 – Getting permission

The first step in this process is to get permission for an email campaign since you are going to be reaching out to a lot of people. For this, your focus should be on constructing a sizeable email list to which you can send your emails.

Some businesses opt for giving something for free, while others tend to offer an update or give a newsletter with information to obtain an email address. However, that is up to you but there are some things you will need to keep in mind if you are going to be asking for an email address. This is going to be the first call to action and simply posting 'enter your email address for updates and latest news' is not going to cut it.

You have to be prepared for questions like "What do I get if I give you my email id?", and "Am I going to get spam emails and will I get discounts?"

To be successful in this phase, focus on being specific. For example, telling when exactly they will receive whatever they are signing up for or what exactly they are going to get.

The second thing is to get whitelisted because try as you may, there is no guarantee if you are going to end up in the inbox folder or the spam or junk folder of a user. Being whitelisted means that your email goes through to the inbox, which only happens if you get saved as a contact address in the user's contact book. Adding instructions to do so in your email, especially on the first email is important to ensure that the following emails you send are not missed or overlooked. Keep in mind that being whitelisted means or is equal to being marked as a friend.

There are hardly any users that go out of their way to remove people from their emailing lists, so this is an almost sure shot-way of ensuring your email never gets marked as spam or you get on the blacklist monitor. You can even take a look at instructions from some of the most popular email service providers like Mailchimp and AWeber.

Step 2 – Do the math

The second phase is all about playing the numbers game. What this means is that you have to manage the expectations you set with your emails with constant follow up efforts. Anything you do is going to remain nothing with any follow up activity and especially in email marketing, it is all about expectations. This in no way means that if you promised to send one email a week, but you end up sending emails daily, because even that will get a negative response. Like with everything else you have to pace yourself. It works the other way around, for example, if you have set the expectation of a user to get emails from you daily about important updates, but then you do not deliver on that promise then that essentially means your service is lousy.

This is also the reason why the first follow up email you send is so crucial because it becomes a deciding factor for most of the clients. Amongst the email service provider that you are going to be using, the majority of them have the option of creating an autoresponder sequence so it is a good idea to take advantage of them.

The first follow up email that you send is the best way to introduce yourself and your business more deliberately along with explaining what it is exactly that you plan on doing with the email address of your client. In this case it is a better option to be detailed and specific rather than opt for being quick and unobtrusive, because this is the best opportunity to get the client hooked because after this, it is only a game of living up to the client's expectations.

As I mentioned the use of an auto responder before, the advantage I found in it is that if you often forget to email your list. Unless you have something to sell then this is where you can be saved because let's face it, you are going to forget and that is also not the ideal situation. You can program content and schedule it to be sent over a basis of a few months consistently through an auto responder. The added pro here is that when you do need to get in touch with your client base about something new, you will not be coming out of the blue, because you will already have been in touch with the clientele. You will have built a relationship by consistently being in touch. This will also annoy your email readers and clients less because it will not seem that you only pop up with emails when you want to do business or have something to sell. Just be sure to schedule your autoresponder not to send too many emails.

Step 3 – Segmentation and analysis

This is the last concrete stage of running an email marketing campaign and the most important one as well since most marketers do not do this thoroughly. Analytics is important in every online aspect and every service provider provides complementary analytics. There are various types of analytics but the most important ones I have found to be are open rates, click through rates and unsubscribes. The open rate tells you how successful you have been in building a relationship. So if the number is low then that means the people you send emails to have started to delete the emails upon receiving them. This signals that you need to work on providing better value and managing expectations so that your emails are opened.

For the click through rate, a lower number means that either the message you are trying to get across is not targeted enough or is simply being obstructed by a barrier. The last type of analytics is more serious if the number is high or has changed. Getting a high unsubscribe rate shows that people are actually opting out of receiving your emails. They are actually going through the trouble of not having to delete the emails by simply not getting them. This shows that you have some serious work to do in terms of taking action and retaining clients based on those leaks. Maybe you can get more information about why they are leaving and try to fix the problem.

Re-work the way you present your messages, re work your call to action and the auto responder emails. If you pay attention to email analytics, then you can end up finding out where the problem lies in your email funnel since they can give you very specific clues about where you might be going wrong.

On another note based on the same stage, segmentation also comes in to play here. Basically, segmentation means splitting up your client list on the basis of relevant details in to smaller groups that you can target more specifically and cater to with more attention. By splitting the list, you are giving yourself the opportunity to have more targeted communication with your clients and build a more meaningful relationship.

You can also learn over time what certain customers want. Some may only want to know about new versions of your services and products, while others may want to hear about promotions and offers by your company. Giving them a chance to choose between they want to hear from you may translate to you losing them altogether. For example, through segmentation you can also specifically send an email to those customers who did not open your last message and give them a second pitch.

Chapter 10
Offline Marketing

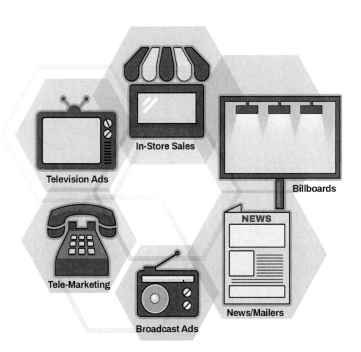

In-Store Sales

Television Ads

Billboards

Tele-Marketing

Broadcast Ads

News/Mailers

Not much has been talked about yet one of the most trending marketing methods in the previous years. Offline marketing has been a big part of every industry for many decades before the Internet became mainstream. However, there are people who are unaware of offline marketing or at least have not tried it for their business because online marketing has become the new normal. Now, offline marketing is not even an option if you want to compete with other businesses.

Offline marketing consists of traditional methods in the field of marketing, such as printing pamphlets, running advertisements on television, putting up billboard signs, and many more which will be discussed in this chapter.

The world has progressed at a much faster pace and everything has revolutionized now. From the method of marketing the product to the quality and other aspects of the product, everything has changed a lot in the recent years. In the previous years, there was no such thing as a telephone, but now everyone has a smartphone, which has reduced the use of many other forms of communication. Everything is now available in one smartphone. Now, you do not need to carry a calculator, a notepad, a camera, or a flashlight. Similarly, there are several other things that have been revolutionized, and so did the way of marketing them.

If you want to understand what offline marketing means, here is a formal definition: Offline marketing strategies utilize offline media channels to create awareness of a company's product, regardless of its nature. The offline channels include telemarketing strategies such as adverts on television, radio, and print media (pamphlets and billboards). However, we are going to discuss the majorly used offline marketing methods in detail.

Network/Contacts

Initially, when launching a website or getting started with traffic, one of the best-suited ways is face-to-face communication with your business contacts or the people you know. Telling them about your website and your business can help build up their interest and they may want to visit your website and refer it to the people they know.

Though speaking individually to a group of people may not get you any far, but trying to approach and seeking opportunities to speak with your field-related gathering may get you some interested customers that could create a deeper sense of brand loyalty among all of your customers. It is one of the most old-fashioned ways of marketing yet it is quite effective and very cost efficient. It hardly costs anything to speak up about your brand with a group of people who work in your field of work. Despite having so many new ways to market your product, you still have a clear shot at getting a bunch of interested customers through this method.

Speaking Engagements

This method is quite similar to the previous one we have talked about. In this method as well, you have to speak up about your product and make people interested in what you are selling or providing to them. Through this method, you can try and choose bigger platforms to speak about your product. Take seminars for example, or exhibitions where the majority of the people roaming around belong to the related fields.

Apart from this, there are several other reasons why speaking engagements are better. The first reason is that speaking engagement actually puts you right in front of the target customer and gives you a chance to speak about your product in front of a highly targeted and interested audience. Before you even utter a single word, they are already prepared to listen carefully to every word you say and pay attention to detail of what you are going to brief on.

It is also believed that speaking engagements are one of the greatest ways to build credibility and leadership within your firm. However, there is one thing that you need to keep in mind before opting for this strategy. Since speaking in front of a large and highly interested crowd could be a really tough challenge, it is advised to find and start off with local associations and small crowds to build up confidence.

Along with confidence being a challenge, you are less likely to have any contacts who would refer you in huge seminars with crowds in the beginning. Take your time, build up your confidence and your contacts, so you can benefit the most from this old-school method.

Cold Calls

It is one of the long-forgotten methods, yet it is highly-effective. Looking at the volume of this method being used while pitching for sales, some people might feel that cold calling is actually dead, but I think not. It cannot be that bad or old to consider it almost dead or even on the verge of extinction. It sounds quite funny, but cold calls have their own touch and there is a high chance that they can resonate at a high rate with interested buyers. Phone calls placed to old clients could be a much more effective way than contacting through email. Besides, phone calls demand instant responses, unlike emails where the customers can take several days to respond or sometimes even forget about it.

Before approaching your old clients, just remember that they are one of your most potential customers and you cannot afford to lose them. Once they lose their interest in you, it can become a trouble for you to deal with. One important thing to remember while contacting them is the time. Try to figure out when would be the best time to approach them. Do not consider calling them after their office hours. There is a huge possibility they would get pissed off and you will eventually end up losing them.

Apart from being a great way to approach your old customers, the cold calls can also help you get in touch with people interested in collaborating with your business. You may find potential business partners through cold calls and it could be a great step for you toward progress. Take your time and dig out your old contacts, you never know what awaits you.

Print Publications

Print publications are still a valuable way of marketing and are still in use by some businesses. If you are lucky enough to obtain valuable and interesting places in relevant magazines, journals, and newspapers, you are going to get a high number of people for your product.

There's no denying the fact that print publications highlight your brand visibility and area of expertise. Make sure to look for as many opportunities as you could for print publications to increase your brand visibility and brand awareness. Don't just go around publishing everywhere. It could be a waste of your capital. Seek out every opportunity but only avail the ones that seem relevant and beneficial to you. You have to be highly-selective in this method.

Also, remember to try your best to target only the interested audience through print publications method. Even though you are never going to be 100% accurate it can lead to good results.

Trade Shows/Associations

Trade shows are one of the best ways to approach the people of similar interests and fields. There is a high chance that trade shows are likely to be filled with industry-related leaders and potential buyers that are ready to place orders upfront. Trade shows entail not only placing a little stall or handing out goodies but also taking orders in bulk and growing your business on a higher level.

It is safe to say that this is the most effective offline marketing method ever to exist. Networking, print publications, and speaking engagements: nothing compares to the results obtained from this method alone. If we look at this method from a general perspective, it is a sum of several other methods that makes it simply the most effective one. It includes networking and speaking engagements because you communicate with people in person. Also, you have a clear opportunity to hand out your printed publications to those people, so they can read more about your product and develop their interest.

Print Advertising

Lastly, print advertising is quite similar to print publications, except for the fact that you market your product directly instead of printing articles on pamphlets or leaflets. Print advertising also includes putting up huge billboards on top of buildings to insure that people see what you are selling. It is one of the least preferred or high investment-requiring methods, yet quite effective as compared to running adverts on television.

The biggest drawback of this method, it could be a tough challenge to track the turnover of people being interested in your product after looking at billboards.

Uses of Offline Marketing

Offline marketing could be the most effective way to approach the people who are not very active on the web. People who are more dedicated toward their business and do not look forward to being reached out to online, can be contacted via offline marketing strategies stated above. These methods are not that much outdated and are still used on a big scale. All of the billboards, pamphlets, and printed publications are still used by many business owners and representatives.

Here is one major benefit of using offline marketing method. Consider you are going to fetch groceries from a nearby store and on your way down, you think of all the things you need. There is a possibility that you may encounter a few billboards just before the store or mart - billboards of necessities such as meat or bread that you might be forgetting. Coming across those billboards on your way to the mart will increase the chances of you going out to pick the same product of the same manufacturer you just saw on the billboard instead of any other. This is how a firm may benefit from this method of offline marketing.

Luckily, there is no need to choose between online and offline marketing. Both can operate harmoniously at the same time. Offline marketing cannot replace online marketing methods and vice versa.

We will be looking into the summary to glance back at everything we have discussed and to insure brief understanding with readers. Clearly understanding and implementing the right strategies can enable the readers to utilize every aspect of this book to its full potential. After all, the purpose of this book is to serve as a guide and tool for those who are entering the world of business or those who are already experienced in this particular field.

Chapter 11

Customer Relationship Managers (CRMs)

Once you have taken in and digested most of the grand scheme of the digital marketing techniques and methods we have gone through in the previous chapters, you may fall into two pools of people. One is of a person who puts everything into practice, and has done so at such precision and success, that you are able to coach, consult, and thus share with people your own experience and vision for success on the digital marketing front.

The second pool you may fall into is someone who sees the importance and value of implementing each of these methods, but simply doesn't have the time or willpower to be working on these methods regularly. In this case, perhaps you should seek out a consultant.

In essence, if the survival of your business is dependent on your full attention, and does not allow time for marketing efforts, it is advisable you look into hiring and perhaps retaining a marketing consultant. Many businesses require constant tending to, creativeness, research and development that may not afford the time to engage in such activities. You never know, your hyper-focused prowess and proficiency in what you give to the market could one day be worth a big ticket consultation or speaking engagement.

My Journey as a Consultant

Although I often am a practicing technician in digital marketing, I have always been sought after in some form as a consultant. In my early years before heading my agency, I served as an in house consultant for a financial house. Years after, I launched a consultancy out of a small office in Van Nuys, California, in which small business owners from around the area would get advice and help with marketing their website. If they didn't have one, our small team would be glad to help.

Due to our collective proficiency in websites and digital marketing, we were able to grow in the size of our clients, and we were able to move out of that constrained little office in the San Fernando Valley.

As we worked to market our newly established Websites Depot brand, the client list grew and became more diverse. In 2019, I am proud to say that it has grown immensely, and my calendar is fully booked with 1-on-1 consultations with my clients. We've achieved a level of growth that I am grooming.

How To Carry Yourself As a Consultant

My foremost and most simplest advice as to how to deal with your consulting clients is to show empathy. Relate to your client and find out what makes them tick. If you are a career digital marketing specialist, then find out how business is doing, how about some insights on sales?

It's important to ask plenty of questions in order to get on the same level with them. Keep it a bit informal at first and just dig into some very general information. It will allow you to match mood and tone and be relatable, making their time and money worthwhile.

Also, find out what is their key performance indicators, if they have any. If they don't have any, perhaps tell them to take some time in the next few days to think of some. This will help you determine the metric in which they will be able to judge you by both in your consultation and well into the future. Is

it sales volume? Average sale price? Web traffic?
Social media likes? Quality content? It really could be
a range of things, so it's best to find out.

Speaking Engagements

You may get to a point in which you're fairly
sought after as a consultant. In this point, you may
be even more effective in offering consultation to the
masses. It's important not to get ahead of yourself
however, as a speaker, you have to have established
credibility in your profession over the years.

I kind of equate the speaking circuit to being
a DJ-- in the beginning stages, you may have to make
an investment, or even have to pay a venue-- to get
your foot in the door. You may even be charged
with having to sell tickets to your own event. Indeed,
this is how some speakers start off. There are some
exceptions however, and these are for individuals that
have excelled in their field--- for example, famous poli-
ticians, businessmen, celebrities, and academics.

For example, Hillary Clinton and Elon Musk
get paid a fortune to speak to some very exclusive
crowds about their "inside" knowledge of their line of
work. But this is because they are A-list celebrities
in their own right. Their going rate is not something
that is common in the speaking world, so most gurus
and aspiring speakers fall into the column of starters.
So practice your speaking, and your sharing of inside
knowledge on whatever it is that you do, but keep
your expectations tempered until you have a solid
establishment within the speaking circuit(s).

My advice for starters is to pick your speaking engagements wisely, look for opportunities that don't end up breaking your bank. Once you book an event, then market it full force! Refer back to previous chapters, if needed. And let people know on your Facebook, Eventbrite, Twitter, and email blasts what an opportunity it will be to hear you speak. You do, after all, have a wealth of knowledge to share. For more on speaking engagements and how to handle them, refer to the offline marketing chapter of this book.

Public speaking should be phased out in a way that you have enough of a credibility that potential attendees will know you have something to offer. I've recently embarked on this journey, but I am still strategically finding ways to find clever placement for those who will listen.

Public speaking could be a great way to form a side stream of revenue. Much like Elon Musk does, he has an existing booking page for his speaking engagements. Of course, this is not what he does on a daily basis, as he's busy running a dynamic car company and a space program at the same time! This also goes back to compliment you in your online reputation efforts. If you have videos, speaking pages, written volumes, then you in effect will own the prime real estate that is the first page of your name search. Serious business people should pay plenty of focus and effort into your company's name, and your name as an individual.

I recently spoke at the Los Angeles small business expo, and my team did a great job reeling people in from throughout the venue. The result was a few attendees inquiring about consultation, and a well-lite, well-shot YouTube video that provides about an hour worth of inside knowledge on digital marketing. The turnout ended up being good and lively.

Do You Need a Consultant?

There are a few ways to determine this, depending on what stage your business is in. Those in the early stages of their business life cycle may need some advice and coaching on how to scale their business and phase out investment, especially in marketing in a way that doesn't stunt growth.

Established businesses may need an outside consultant to come in and take a look at the internal dynamics of things. I find that in this case fewer business owners or principal proprietors come to me, but rather heads of marketing departments. In some cases, an entire team seeks me out for some insights of what to do. Sometimes it does become increasingly difficult to gauge proper goals and performance indicators, because each may be putting attention on their own metrics. In this case it's good to get a feel for who is the key decision maker of the bunch, in order to know who to defer to in deciding the direction of which to take.

Consulting With Small businesses

It's important to establish with the head of a small business that there is no overnight fix to stagnant or slow growth. Sure, you can throw some ad money at the issue and it can generate you new business, but the right approach for longstanding and steady growth is a healthy mix of each of the things that we've discussed in the previous pages. Perseverance is key.

When speaking to heads of small businesses, it's important to temper expectations and delusions of grandeur. The track to success in the case of most successful businesses takes carefully coordinated phases. Whether you're a consultant or the consultee, you'll need to take inventory of where the business is at the time. How much capital does it have to work with? How big is the workforce? What are the overhead costs? Even for a digital marketing expert, all these things should be closely pondered. For those receiving consultation, be forthcoming. You don't have to give away a closely-kept business model or a secret formula, but let a consultant know what the aches and pains are in the business. Don't seek only quick fixes, but perhaps substantial changes that can be made to help you level up as a business.

Searching for the Right Consultant

Do your research. If you have a very niche industry, I suggest you seek out someone who caters to that, or someone who has worked in that industry and has become a consultant. If you need help with digital marketing, and you're in the U.S., Websites Depot is always just a phone call away. There are many great consultants out there, so be sure to call around and get a feel for those which might be right for you. I'll hold myself up to the best of them, so feel free to inquire within. as a side note, if you'd like to find out more about my 1-on-1 consulting, or my insights, visit DannyStar.com or WebsitesDepot.com.

Not all of those will be savvy to the digital marketing world, however. So it is often commonplace that medium to large businesses will seek out multiple consultants. Regardless of who you may choose, it's important to find information about them online and get a second opinion. This includes review sites and also a background check on the consultant, if available. If one is not available, this could raise a red flag. If you're able to find a YouTube introduction, even better. For those who aspire to coach or consult, do yourself a favor and film yourself giving a short introduction, or a small taste of your insights to the world. This serves to give you credibility in the eyes of perspective clients.

How Does Consulting Work For A Business?

Getting the proper business consultation will allow businesses of any size to get a second look at their internal workings. It's a good way to take a look under the hood, so to speak. All too often a single diagnosis of how a marketing campaign can be improved is simply insufficient. As a rule of thumb, I have always told stakeholders in businesses that a healthy marketing budget is equivalent to about 10 percent of gross revenues. But where do you go from there? How to split the pie of that remainder of the ten percent. There is no one-size-fits-all answer, and the best way to gather the proper prescription is to ask a pertinent series of questions that will help you reach that proper diagnosis.

In some cases, a serious look at approaches to merchandising and ad budgets must be had. I have found that in my years of digital marketing consultations with various business owners, most have had their digital ads programmed in ways that burn holes right through their pocket books.

Of course, if you're not a digital marketing expert, but are acting as a consultant, you'll have to be privy to a business wasting too much money on a certain department. If this is the case in the marketing department, then perhaps a digital marketing expert, rather than a traditional marketing expert, could be 'just what the doctor ordered.'

Sometimes the heads of business may feel that they are engaging in marketing all in vain. In many cases, it only takes a bit of advice, or just a few adjustments, to begin to turn a corner. In cases in which I step in, it's only a matter of beginning to diversify a marketing portfolio. In other words, putting the many topics in the previous chapters into play. What that does is begin to bring in new channels of information that will give feedback and will eventually reveal a place to focus marketing efforts and budgets.

Consulting Vs. Coaching

It's not too much of a distinguishment. Consulting is done in a bit of a more of an informal setting. Normally it's scheduled during office hours. Coaching takes on a bit of a less formal approach, and involves a bit of following around and practicing. It's no mistake it takes on a sports connotation. Sometimes there are corrections to be made when honing digital skills that need to be made on the fly. Coaching could entail getting to know a new cloud-based program, CRM, platform, or technology.

Clearly, consulting is writing up a prescription for long term growth. If we must have to look into what is necessary to survive, we're not ready to have a discussion about what is necessary to thrive quite yet-- although this is the ultimate goal.

Common Advice for Consultants & Consultees

Take what you can that's free out there. In the digital age, you have access to countless videos, writings and free seminars that you can partake in on the web. Given the seamless delivery of content in the broadband age, you are able to access all of this quickly and cheaply. Pick up on consultation tips, and watch great speakers and their mannerisms that help guide conversations and wow those who listen. In many cases, to retain a new customer, you'll have to wow them and present to them something they feel they might not get anywhere else.

Another way to spread your influence is to be present at other speaking engagements. Here you'll get a chance to meet speakers and other luminaries. In many cases, especially in more informal settings, many people you meet will be more than glad to share their insights. In other words, get out there and network, share business cards, and maybe find some common ground in which you can work together.

If you aspire to consult and coach, this could be a very viable extra source of income for you. Use every resource you can to gain ideas and inspiration of how to become better in your craft. Find your niche-- are you a better phone consultant? Are you better speaking and presenting? Or perhaps you're more data driven, and would prefer to present reports and figures. It doesn't matter which of these you are, do it in a way that is empathetic to your subjects who are giving you their time. This was my first bit of advice in this chapter.

In our digital marketing industry, it's always important to be keeping tabs on new platforms, methods, and technologies that are evolving and becoming as useful as ever. In many cases, you'll hear about it through a peer in the industry.

For industry outsiders, a digital marketing guru, or specialist, or agency can help introduce you to some of the latest and greatest business boosting online tools and products on the market.

Chapter 12

In Summary &
In Parting

Much like my career has been up to this point, putting together this book has been nothing short of a journey through a vast array of time-tried experiences.

I have a small bit of advice for both aspiring marketers to season professionals, and from small startups to thriving entrepreneurs: take the journey and relish it. I discourage the practice of looking out into the horizon, thinking that there is going to be a magical one-day fix to digital marketing success. It's a curated process and there's no singular way of doing it, so in a way, it is an art form.

Success will ultimately be achieved through your time and persistence that you invest into this journey. You may want to invest money to help the cause of your digital marketing. In this case, call up a guru, or better yet, contact a reputable web agency to work on your behalf. I always advise my clients that it's like putting great minds together, all for one cause. For this, you must choose your team wisely. So please do your due diligence and your research into the experience, reputation, and track record of any web agency you come across.

What's great about the dynamics of digital marketing, is that you can work with a countless amount of people from all over the planet. This is a special time in this world in which small business owners have an immense amount of power right at their fingertips-- so you should rest assured exercise them! Know that by using a good mix of the aforementioned tactics, you will be able to reap excellent benefits in the future in the form of revenue for your business. In summary of what we learned in this book-- let's revisit and see how it all comes together:

We've discussed how Digital Marketing came to be what it is now with the evolution of the Internet. It's not the same as it was-- say, even a few months ago. It's constantly evolving, so we must evolve with it. It may have snuck up on the traditionalist marketers, but it is now here to stay and it is now the prominent form of marketing.

One of the major methods of marketing today, because of the large user base, is SEO. We discussed which tools and tactics work best. At the forefront is the quality of your original content-- be pertinent to what you sell and cater to those looking for what you have to offer. Make it easy for them to find you. Believe me, that if they find you easy to find on a search, they will remember your name by heart the next time they are in need of your product or service.

Content is king, but do make use of the tools to make sure that your business and your website is easily searchable. This includes speed tests, SEO tests, test runs on your phone to improve mobile experience, and so on. Make sure you give someone who lands on your site a seamless experience. And don't confuse a seamless experience with aesthetic appeal, as we distinguished in the later chapters where we covered design.

Remember that relevance is key for appearing in searches. Does your content have authority to answer questions posed by potential customers? You should pose those questions every day when building your business profiles and contributing to your website. Represent your business interests in as many platforms as are offered, then tend to them. That is how you build your presence over time.

After we covered that part-- this you should be searchable by now. Maybe not at the top quite yet, but searchable nonetheless. This is your time to phase in your reputation management. Build a buzz about yourself, and create partnerships and relationships with those who will create a buzz online for you. Build links to your websites and tie them in with relevant information that is valuable to your consumer base. Encourage your customers to write you a review or give a shout out on social media. Each of these small things can go a long way in the overall scope of things.

Beyond building that which is positive, be vigilant against any negative stuff that comes up about your or your business. If you are not vigilant, negative posts tend to multiply because they get cited or mentioned elsewhere. When this happens, it could fill up a top SERP page with multiple pages that don't help your business cause. In this case, you may need to engage in a very deeply rooted reputation management campaign. This could require work of professionals. The cheapest and most efficient way to manage and build is by engaging in "preventative care."

Part of putting your "best foot forward" ahead of competitors, can be helped by engaging in PPC. If you are a startup, then discretion in your budget is key. Larger companies have more to play with, and many are already engaging in PPC in some form.

This is the fastest way to appear on first page search results, but it's very important that the budget is being monitored with the progress. Be sure you are careful in configuring your ad setups, and if need be, seek help from a professional.

PPC affords you platforms that move fast and are dynamic-- all available to give you marketing feedback in real time. A healthy way to go about a digital marketing campaign would be to have a healthy balance of organic SEO efforts coupled with strategic paid marketing. Putting these two things together will tie into the greater theme that is revealed at the end of this summary.

Dynamic advertising can also be executed on social media platforms, but this must be done after your social media profiles are established and optimized. Take the time to nurture your social media profile, and engage with people directly to make a following. After that, you'll be able to convince more people to take action on your advertising campaigns.

Also, remember just how much social media factors into your search engine optimization. Be sure to link frequently back to your site by offering. In summary of what I said in my social media section, take the time to master each platform individually--- don't burden yourself on too many accounts all at one time. Master one, then move on to the other. This will give you the biggest payoff in the end.

Do all these things, then you will have achieved a good following. But don't rest on your laurels. Once you have a good funnel of traffic coming into your website and inquiring about you, offer them a bit more of information for exchange of their email addresses. Studies have now shown that direct email marketing has some of the best returns on investment.

Building a list does take time, however. I strongly discourage purchasing lists of emails that have never opted in to receive your information. Doing so can get you blocked as an email sender in many instances. Collect email addresses on your website in exchange for an ebook or free strategy session, a free cupcake, etc. By doing this you'll be able to contact them in the future with promotional information like your best deals, new products, coupons, and more.

An email inbox is a very personal space, so to have invited you in grants you a bit of intimacy and trust from the get go. Take advantage of the situation-- but don't be too pushy. By pushy I mean sending out a hailstorm of emails every month. Take time to formulate a clever message, a new design, then look at the analytics of how it performed. This will put you in position for the next email blast. Also, make use of a service that enables you to distribute in bulk, and also protects your server identity. MailChimp, Constant Contact, and HubSpot right now serve as great places to design an email and distribute it to your entire list.

Although digital marketing is the prominent form of marketing, one must not discount the effectiveness of offline marketing. After all, a personal conversation or an in person demonstration can have much more of an impression on a potential customer. Keep in mind how effective it would be if you engaged in speaking arrange-ments, or held one-on-one consults? The drawback of this marketing is not in it's effectiveness, but rather it's reach, which is quite limited. Practice this with good discretion, but do value your personal time.

Considering all of the things we've gone over

in these volumes, my final advice is to use them in tandem. Depending on your industry, one of these methods may prove to help you more than others, but each of these methods will serve to contribute to your bottom line cumulatively, especially when executed properly.

For those interested in Digital Marketing who are not in the business world-- be sure to define your goals, no matter what they are-- and define them into something that is measurable. For professionals and business owners-- have clear set goals as well. Determine what your key performance indicators are, then test the vehicles discussed in this book to see which one achieves the most for you. This applies whether you are selling food, tickets, clothing, hardware, cleaning services-- whatever the case. Make use of the tracking methods described in this book, and you'll be able to track your key metrics easily.

Work hard, stay dedicated, and enjoy the journey.

Additional Resources
For the latest news and trends:
SearchEngineLand.com
Searh Engine Journal

Auditing Tools:
SEMRush.com -- SEO Keyword Analysis
SEO Toobox -- https://toolbox.seositecheckup.com/
    -- this is a comprehensive site audit.
SEO Expert Report- https://seoexpertreport.com/
    -- A more intuitive SEO audit.
Moz -- https://moz.com/
    -- A tool for monitoring backlinks & their sources.

For Education:
Google Ads Academy
https://SEO.Academy

46793275R00082

Made in the USA
San Bernardino, CA
08 August 2019